HOLDING NOTHING BACK

Dedication

To my gorgeous wife, Rachel.
Sharing this life with you is my greatest joy.
I love you with all my heart.

Holding Nothing Back

TIM HUGHES

survivor

Unless otherwise indicated Bible quotations are from
the New International Version © 1973, 1978, 1984
by the International Bible Society.

Thankyou Music songs adm. by
worshiptogether.com songs excl. UK and Europe
adm. by Kingswaysongs.com (tym@kingsway.co.uk)

ISBN 978 184291 352 9

Survivor is an imprint of
KINGSWAY COMMUNICATIONS LTD
Lottbridge Drove, Eastbourne BN23 6NT, England.
Email: info@survivor.co.uk

Printed in Great Britain

Contents

Acknowledgements

There were many people involved who made this book possible.

I'm hugely grateful to those who diligently read through various chapters making insightful and helpful comments; particularly my wife Rachel (you were amazingly patient and thoughtful, regularly ploughing through the manuscript with me late into the night), Mum and Dad, my brothers Peter and Stephen, Al Gordon and Rob Bewley. Will Jackson – thanks for researching and finding all those great facts!

All at Kingsway/Survivor, especially Les Moir, Richard Herkes and Carolyn Owen.

Thanks for all the hard work you put into this book.

All at Regal Books, USA, especially Bill & Rhonnie Greig and Alex Field. You've constantly encouraged and challenged me to write this book. Thank you for your patience when I continually pushed back the deadline!

Thank you to those leaders, preachers and teachers who have inspired and refined my thinking over the years, Dad, Mike Pilavachi, Nicky Gumbel, Ken Costa, Graham Tomlin, Matt Redman, David Ruis, Don Williams and Louie Giglio.

To my family and friends around the world who faithfully love, support and pray for me.

Foreword

I first met Tim at Soul Survivor back in 1998. I was in the crowd of 6000 young people gathered into a ramshackle, tin-roofed building, worshipping God as though it was the last night on earth. The biggest youth event to emerge in Britain over the last 20 years, Soul Survivor has always been known as an intimate yet powerful place of worship for thousands of kids throughout the UK. Each one taking their own personal pilgrimage to the Shepton Mallet showground in the West Country, to go deeper with God and discover what it can be like if you give your life over to a living God.

So here I stood, with my wife Anna and our kids, listening to a young man lead his 'congregation' into the presence of God. The term 'presence of God' is a phrase that is a little over-used these days, but still accurate and beautiful. Tonight we were in this very 'presence' of God, and I'll never forget the tenderness and strength with which Tim led us. You can have a coach full of people all wanting to go somewhere, but unless there is a driver the bus won't leave and it certainly won't arrive. As a worship leader your job is to sit in the driver's seat and occasionally touch the steering wheel of a vehicle that is already moving. Hold it too hard and you go off course; hold it too lightly and you end up going round the car park in circles.

Tim is a man of his time, dedicated to seeing the glory of God in the nations. Dedicated to training others in what he has learnt. Dedicated to the craft of songwriting. And dedicated to being a husband and dad.

What I have learnt over the years is that there is more to Tim that meets the eye. King David was not just a king but a prophet, a musician, a strategist and a skilled businessman. Tim has all these attributes and more.

Everywhere I travel around the world, in all the continents, people of every creed and colour are singing the songs that have been penned by this man. I feel like a proud older brother who stands back in awe and amazement at what he has achieved. God certainly knew what he was doing when he called this young lad out of obscurity to be a leader of a nation.

To God be the glory, great things he has done, and great things he will continue to do. Read this book and learn to fly.

Tim Hughes: the best is yet to come.

Martin Smith

April 2007

Foreword

We all have a theology – in some ways we are all theologians. Whether or not we are conscious of it, or can articulate it clearly, we all believe *something* about God. Even the atheist believes enough to have formed the opinion that he doesn't believe at all.

How we *see* God. . . how we perceive him through the lens of our knowledge and experience . . . greatly affects both the expression and walking out of our faith in worship. Liturgy, in all its forms, is shaped by the basic building blocks of how we have come to know God. From the austere to the more exuberant and spontaneous expressions of worship – right across the spectrum of the worshipping church – theology shapes liturgy; and possibly even more importantly, in many cases the worship experience can shape the theology.

The latter is probably truer than ever in the times in which we live. In recent years there has been a surge of the popularity and exposure of contextualized worship (especially music) that is more contemporary with the secular culture. More than ever, common songs are being sung across denominational lines, and the flavours of most church cultures have become much more relaxed and akin to each other – mainly through the effect of the current worship movement. Mix this with the lack of Bible knowledge both inside and outside the church, and the primary means of people forming their opinions about who God is, is largely through the songs we sing and the atmosphere that we create when we gather together.

This poses a great challenge to the worshipping church.

Tim brings a timely and clear message that we all need to hear. We must *know* God . . . with *all* of our heart, strength, soul and mind. This is not just something for the head, nor is it only for the heart. It is a call for theological integrity in liturgy *and* in lifestyle.

As the church continues in its ongoing journey of learning how to express eternal worship in a temporal world of constant flux and change, it faces a critical issue: how to foster a desire for a holistic worship that recognises the awe that the knowledge of the Holy inspires, without losing the intimate reality of 'drawing near' in the worshipper's journey. Just as importantly, we must engage a theology that is not content to stay within the walls of the church structure but affects the world by bringing this knowledge of God to the last, the least and the lost.

Let's heed Tim's call to us to cultivate worshipping lifestyles that are secure in the sovereignty of a mighty God and the love that allows us to open our hearts before him. Standing on the solid ground of truth, we can freely express our faith and love. From the lament to the exuberant shout of praise, let the church sing her songs, and engage her world with a faith that holds nothing back.

David Ruis

1
You are above and beyond understanding...

We all gathered for the start of the conference. Expectant and excited for a day of worship and teaching, we eagerly waited for the first session to start. As the worship leader sat down at the piano, we all stood, obedient and well-trained churchgoers, and waited to be led. With his eyes shut, clearly already in the zone, the worship leader began speaking out. 'How are You doing today God? What's on Your mind? What's consuming Your thoughts? Are You worried about anything today God? What's getting You down?' This was definitely different from most of the calls to worship I had been involved in. Caught in this moment, our worship-leader friend carried on, 'What are You up to today God? Are You looking after the starving child in Africa, or are You helping the stressed out mum find her car keys so that she can get her kids to school on time?' At this we all began to look at each other, somewhat puzzled and perplexed.

I'll be honest, it was not the greatest start to a worship time. Rather than being filled with awe and amazement at the strength and might of the Sovereign Lord, I began to panic that He might be having a crisis of confidence. Maybe God needed a rest, some time out. I mean, He has been going at it full belt for quite a while now. Before I allowed this line of thinking to get out of control, I stopped myself and thought, isn't God everywhere? Isn't He all-powerful? Isn't He eternal? Isn't He all-knowing and unchanging? In our time of worship we had been dumbing God down to our earthly level. We had been trying to relate to Him as 'our good old mate round the corner'. We had forgotten the otherness of God. He is transcendent and glorious, above and beyond understanding.

A. W. Tozer, in his classic book *The Knowledge of the Holy* writes, 'The Church has surrendered her once lofty concept of God and has substituted for it one so low, so ignoble as to be utterly unworthy of thinking, worshipping men.'[1]

The Church needs to recapture a big picture of all that God is. Our view and understanding of Him will have a significant impact on our worship. As Graham Kendrick says, 'Worship is a response and will grow or shrink in direct proportion to our view of Him.'[2] So, let's dig a bit deeper and press on into the mystery and character of God.

You terrify, yet welcome in

It was one of the most majestic and terrifying sights I'd ever seen: about ten metres from our car was a large pride of lions,

[1] A. W. Tozer, *The Knowledge of the Holy*, HarperCollins, 1961, p.vii

[2] Quoted from www.harvestsongs.org

lying out in the blazing African sun. My heart was beating hard and perspiration was beginning to pour down my face. After a couple of minutes I was keen to move on. Really keen to move on! Unfortunately for me, however, I happened to be sharing a 4 × 4 with an over-zealous photographer! It soon became apparent that a few snaps out of the window just weren't going to suffice, so before long he was climbing onto the roof and asking the driver to rev the engine in the hope that the lions might start moving; not something that I was very keen to see happen! As one of the lions rose to its feet and stared in our direction, I had never felt so small and vulnerable. This magnificent animal stood there utterly fearless. Looking back, I am so glad we stayed, but at the time I was hugely relieved when we eventually moved on.

In Hosea, there is a verse that at first seems very strange. 'They will follow the Lord; he will roar like a lion. When he roars, his children will come trembling from the west.'[3] In most scenarios when a lion roars, all run for cover. No one in his right mind messes about with a roaring lion. Yet in this picture we see God described as a lion: ferocious, powerful, and kinglike. And when He roars, His children come running towards Him. What a stunning picture. The weakness, fragility and innocence of a child running towards the thing that should terrify and overwhelm her. However, we do not draw near casually. Trembling, we reverently run towards this great God. God's roar is overpowering, intimidating and spectacular, but as we hear it we must run towards Him. Humbly, respectfully and mindfully we need to draw close. He terrifies, yet welcomes in.

---

[3] Hosea 11:10

Augustine writes about the moment when, for the first time, he saw closely the mystery of God, saying that he trembled 'for love and in terror', and that the thought of God made him at once 'shiver and burn with desire'.[4] The psalmist writes, 'You alone are to be feared. Who can stand before you when you are angry?'[5] Yet we later read, 'The LORD is gracious and compassionate, slow to anger and rich in love. The LORD is good to all; he has compassion on all he has made.'[6] We need to embrace these two sides of God, which bring both friendship and fear. So, as Paul exhorts us, in the book of Romans, 'Consider therefore the kindness and sternness of God.'[7] In the same way that we need two eyes in order to enjoy any perception of depth and distance, we also need to grasp and understand these two aspects of God's character to greater understand Him, and ultimately fall more in love with Him.

It is important to remember that God is not made in our image. On the contrary, we are made in His. 'For I am God and not man – the Holy One among you.'[8]

There are many attributes of God's character that we can imitate. We can be loving, we can be faithful, we can be forgiving, we can be good, and we can be comforting. However there are certain aspects of God's nature that we as human beings simply cannot share in; qualities in His character that show Him to be totally 'other'. These incommunicable

---

[4] Quoted in Raniero Cantalamessa, *Come Creator Spirit*, Liturgical Press, 2003, p.10

[5] Psalm 76:7

[6] Psalm 145:8–9

[7] Romans 11:22

[8] Hosea 11:9

attributes set Him apart as God and remind us that we are merely mortal. Wayne Grudem writes,

> The difference between God's being and ours is more than the difference between the sun and a candle, more than the difference between the ocean and a raindrop, more than the difference between the arctic ice cap and a snow flake, more than the difference between the universe and the room we are sitting in: God's being is qualitatively different. No limitation or imperfection in creation should be projected on to our thought of God. He is the creator; all else is creaturely. All else can pass away in an instant; he necessarily exists forever.[9]

Self-existent

As humans we need many things to happen on a daily basis in order to survive. We need a constant supply of oxygen, a regular source of water, as well as certain proteins, vitamins and nutrients. In fact each one of us possesses an armoury of instincts that keeps us alive. If we're too cold, we find shelter and warmth. If we're in pain, we seek help and a cure. To be honest, as humans we're a pretty needy bunch. Within a few hours after birth, many animals are not only feeding but are standing up and walking around. By comparison, human babies are somewhat pathetic. Their only way to survive is by screaming. Babies alter both the pitch and volume of their cry depending on how urgent their need of help is. The louder and more piercing the scream, the quicker the response. In this way a human baby gets all the care and attention it needs to survive.

---

[9] Wayne Grudem, *Bible Doctrine*, InterVarsity Press, 1999, p.72

God does not need us or anything in creation in order to survive and exist. He's the uncreated God, absolutely independent and self-sufficient.

> Before the mountains were born or you brought forth the earth and the world, from everlasting to everlasting you are God.[10]

> The God who made the world and everything in it is the Lord of heaven and earth and does not live in temples built by hands. And he is not served by human hands, as if he needed anything, because he himself gives all men life and breath and everything else.[11]

> . . .for every animal in the forest is mine, and the cattle on a thousand hills. I know every bird in the mountains, and the creatures of the field are mine. If I were hungry I would not tell you, for the world is mine and all that is in it.[12]

These verses put a lot into perspective. Our God does not need us in order to survive and exist, but, remarkably, as His creation we can bring Him enormous joy and pleasure. He is not reliant upon us, yet deeply desires our affection and intimacy. He did not need to create us, but He freely chose to do so. He is complete without us, but chooses to draw near and befriend us. What an amazing God!

Unchangeable

Nothing on the earth is permanent; over time, air, land and sea alter, and living things adapt as best they can. Humans

---

[10] Psalm 90:2

[11] Acts 17:24–25

[12] Psalm 50:10–12

change. We may not like it, but change is impossible to escape. Every second, 15 million blood cells are destroyed in the human body. During a 24-hour period, the average human will breathe 23,040 times. We grow old, we gradually wear out.

Around us the earth's boundaries are in a perpetual state of flux as erosion runs its course. Never has the world been more aware of this as global warming wreaks havoc through tsunamis, flooding, drought and hurricanes. In North America the San Andreas fault, which runs from north to south, is slipping at a rate of about five centimetres per year, causing Los Angeles to move towards San Francisco. Scientists forecast that Los Angeles will be a suburb of the city of San Francisco in about 15 million years!

However, change is not just in the physical realm. Emotionally, our feelings can turn in the blink of an eye. In our media the heroes of yesterday become the villains of today. People are falling in and out of love at an alarming rate. I think of a friend of mine whose life was ripped apart one day when his wife came home to say, 'I don't love you anymore.' I have felt the personal pain of breakdown in relationships. The smiles and pats on the back replaced by aloofness and silence. The wear and tear of life leaves us crushed and exhausted. Our existence becomes guarded and we are cautious of giving freely of ourselves.

What a relief it is to centre our lives around a God who is unchanging. A God who is faithful to the end and whose promises are secure. A God who will never leave nor forsake us. A God who can't lie to us. A God who will never let us go.

In the beginning you laid the foundations of the earth, and the heavens are the work of your hands. They will perish, but you remain; they will all wear out like a garment. Like clothing you will change them and they will be discarded. But you remain the same, and your years never end.[13]

God is not man, that he should lie, nor a son of man, that he should change his mind. Does he speak and then not act? Does he promise and not fulfil?[14]

I the LORD do not change.[15]

We have all experienced the searing pain of loss in some shape or form. We have all been wounded by the reality of change: a breakdown in relationship, the loss of a loved one or the end of a dream. In the midst of such uncertainty we can look to a steadfast God who never changes like shifting shadows; who will never fall in and out of love with us. We are His for eternity. Our names are written on His hand. If He is unchanging, then He will be as reliable tomorrow as He was yesterday and is today.

Eternal

God has no beginning and end. He didn't suddenly begin to exist. He always was. Alpha and Omega, He will never die. The God who was and is and is to come.

The number of his years is unsearchable.[16]

. . .to the only God, our Saviour through Jesus Christ our Lord, be glory, majesty, dominion, and authority, *before all time* and now and forever. Amen.[17]

---

[13] Psalm 102:25–27   [15] Malachi 3:6

[14] Numbers 23:19   [16] Job 36:26 NASB

[17] Jude v.25 NASB (my italics)

With the Lord a day is like a thousand years, and a thousand years is like a day.[18]

Do we have an eternal perspective? Trying to comprehend something that never ends is overwhelming. Everything we know on this earth has a beginning and an end. We are born, we die. We wake up, we go to sleep. God alone is eternal and we could spend a lifetime trying to fathom this incomprehensible truth. As we look to this God whose years are limitless, whose days are unending, we are reminded that we worship a truly vast and glorious God. As man touches God, the finite touches the infinite. While we struggle through this earthly life, we know that one day we will find everlasting joy as we worship the God of eternity face to face.

> Brief life is here our portion,
> Brief sorrow, short lived care;
> The life that knows no ending,
> The tearless life is there.

> There God, our King and Portion,
> In fullness of His grace,
> We then shall see forever,
> And worship face to face.[19]

Omnipresent

All around us, God is present. We cannot escape Him. He is present at every point of space. He is unrestricted by size or

---

[18] 2 Peter 3:8

[19] Bernard of Cluny, quoted in A. W. Tozer, *The Knowledge of the Holy*, Harper-Collins, 1961, p.42

spatial dimensions. God cannot be contained or limited. He is everywhere.

> "Am I only a God nearby," declares the LORD, "and not a God far away? Can anyone hide in secret places so that I cannot see him?" declares the LORD. "Do not I fill heaven and earth?" declares the LORD.[20]

> Where can I go from your Spirit? Where can I flee from your presence? If I go up to the heavens, you are there; if I make my bed in the depths, you are there. If I rise on the wings of the dawn, if I settle on the far side of the sea, even there your hand will guide me, your right hand will hold me fast.[21]

> But will God indeed dwell on the earth? Behold, heaven and the highest heaven cannot contain you; how much less this house which I have built?[22]

When I was growing up, one of my dad's favourite phrases was, 'I've only got two hands.' The great news is that God has all the hands! He can do all things. Turning His attention to one person in need does not mean He has no time to listen to our cries for help. It is never either/or. We are limited, restricted by time. For us there really are never enough hours in the day. Wonderfully, God is not like us.

Indescribable

Robert Webber writes, 'Worship needs to acknowledge the unknowable nature of God who is transcendent and other

---

[20] Jeremiah 23:23–24

[21] Psalm 139:7–10

[22] 1 Kings 8:27 NASB

and dwells in eternal mystery.'[23] There are many other aspects of God's character that we could explore, revealing His divine transcendent nature. He is omniscient, meaning that He is all-knowing, perfect in knowledge. He is omnipotent, meaning that He is all-powerful. We could spend a lifetime studying these attributes and still we would only know Him in part. We could use every word in the dictionary to describe the character of God and yet we would fail to even come close to doing Him justice.

I leave you with these rich and wonderful words from Dr S. M. Lockridge:

He's the King of Righteousness.
He's the King of the Ages.
He's the King of Heaven.
He's the King of Glory.
He's the King of kings and He's the Lord of lords.
That's my King.

Well, I wonder, do you know Him?
My King is a sovereign King.
No means of measure can define His limitless love.
No far seeing telescope can bring into visibility the coastline of His shoreless supply.
No barrier can hinder Him from pouring out His blessings.

He's enduringly strong
He's entirely sincere
He's eternally steadfast
He's immortally graceful

---

[23] Robert Webber in *Exploring the Worship Spectrum*, Zondervan, 2004, p.179

He's imperially powerful
He's impartially merciful

Do you know Him?

He's the greatest phenomenon that has ever crossed the horizon of this world.
He's God's Son.
He's the sinner's Saviour.

He's unique
He's unparalleled
He's unprecedented
He's the loftiest idea in literature
He's the highest personality in philosophy

He supplies strength for the weak.
He's available for the tempted and the tried.
He sympathises and He saves.
He strengthens and sustains.
He guards and He guides.
He heals the sick.
He cleansed the lepers.
He forgives sinners.
He discharges debtors.
He delivers the captive.
His promise is sure.
His life is matchless.
His goodness is limitless.
His mercy is everlasting.
His love never changes.
His Word is enough.
His grace is sufficient.
His reign is righteous and

His yoke is easy and
His burden is light.

I wish I could describe Him to you.
But He's indescribable![24]

---

[24] Taken from the now famous monologue of Dr S. M. Lockridge, Pastor of Calvary Baptist Church in San Diego from 1953 to 1993

2

You opened my eyes to Your wonders anew...

It was the last night of what had been a profound course. Over the ten weeks, every Wednesday, we had gathered together to unpack life's biggest questions. During the Alpha course we had shared our deepest fears and our greatest longings. We had journeyed together and seen some wonderful highs and desperate lows. One of the members of the group had encountered God for the first time in an amazing way, and his world had been turned upside down. It only seemed right to ask him to close our final time together in prayer. His prayer was one of the most stunning things I have ever heard. This brand-new Christian simply prayed, 'God, thank You for being with us. You've met with us in incredible ways. And Jesus, thank You that one day I will see You face to face. And I cannot wait. I cannot wait! Amen.' At this he broke down in tears. This successful, intellectual, City accountant was reduced to tears at his new understanding of God's unceasing love. [1]

---

[1] To find out more about Alpha, visit www.alpha.org

We love because He first loved us. As Paul says in Romans, 'Therefore, I urge you, brothers, in view of God's mercy, to offer your bodies as living sacrifices, holy and pleasing to God – this is your spiritual act of worship.'[2] It is in view of God's mercy that we offer up our bodies. Throughout the Bible it is amazing to see how God reveals Himself to different individuals. Uncreated, all-powerful, self-existent, maker of all things, far above understanding, uncontained, unbreakable, infinite God, meeting small, finite, but-a-breath human. It is not much of a match. Yet time and again we see God reach out His mighty hand to save, encourage, inspire, affirm, challenge, convict, equip and empower.

One of my favourite God-encounters in the Bible is Moses at the burning bush. On the far side of the desert, in the middle of nowhere, Moses was wandering around tending to his father-in-law's sheep. In this mundane moment, something unusual suddenly caught Moses' eye. A burning bush; nothing out of the ordinary in the dry heat of the desert, hardly the event of the century. But there was something different about this burning bush. It kept on burning and burning and burning without actually burning up. This phenomenon was so fascinating that Moses was captivated and decided to investigate further. 'I will now turn aside and see this great sight, why the bush does not burn.'[3] In that moment, beside that burning bush, Moses encountered God and was changed forever. He was consumed by the glory of God.

God is glorious. He is so spectacularly beautiful and majestic that when we catch even the smallest of glimpses we too

---

[2] Romans 12:1

[3] Exodus 3:3 KJV

are captivated. We are forever changed, left undone and lost in wonder. We respond to the overwhelming revelation of an incomprehensible God. Wonder is the basis of worship. Thomas Carlyle, the nineteenth-century philosopher and historian, wrote, 'The man who cannot wonder, who does not habitually wonder and worship, is but a pair of spectacles behind which there is no eye.'[4] As we step aside to inquire more into the mystery and awe of who God is, our hearts are captured. The more we look, the more we find. If you look at the night sky, you could count approximately 3,000 stars. Look through binoculars and you could see thousands more. However if you look through a powerful telescope you can see stars in their billions. As we wait, ponder and muse, we will always discover more of God.

Beautiful one

A few years ago I was on holiday in Australia with a friend. One morning I was reading my Bible when a verse jumped out at me: 'He had no beauty or majesty to attract us to him, nothing in his appearance that we should desire him.'[5] Thinking I had misread the verse I scanned over the words again. Is that correct? Did Jesus, the Son of God, walk upon the earth, displaying no beauty or majesty that would attract us to Him? In Philippians we read that Jesus 'made himself nothing, taking the very nature of a servant, being made in human likeness'.[6] What humility. What sacrifice. The King of the universe

---

[4] Quote from www.simplysharing.com/wonder.htm
[5] Isaiah 53:2
[6] Philippians 2:7

chose to take on the status of a slave and walk upon the earth as a man. If we were to have passed by Him, there would have been nothing about Him physically to cause us to take a second look. And yet Jesus' appeal drew huge crowds. His presence alone was utterly attractive to human beings. Jesus forces us to refine our preconceptions about beauty. And for those of us whose eyes have glimpsed the beauty of Christ, we are forever captivated. Like Moses at the burning bush, we are left transfixed; overwhelmed by such a sight our response is worship. It was out of this revelation that I wrote the song 'Beautiful one'.

> You opened my eyes to Your wonders anew
> You captured my heart with this love.
> Because nothing on earth is as beautiful as You.
>
> Beautiful One I love You
> Beautiful One I adore
> Beautiful One my soul must sing[7]

Recognise and respond

As a result of his determination to spread the Word of God, John was imprisoned on the island of Patmos. One day 'in the Spirit' he heard a voice from behind Him. Turning round to find the source of the voice, he saw a sight that caused his body to fall to the floor as though dead. Such was the magnitude of this vision that John was unable to take it in. Awestruck, John struggled to find the right words to describe

---

[7] Tim Hughes, 'Beautiful one', © 2002 Thankyou Music, tym@kingsway.co.uk. Used by permission.

all that he seen; everything was 'like' something else. Someone 'like a son of man'. His head and hair were white 'like
wool', His eyes were 'like blazing fire' and His voice was 'like
the sound of rushing waters'. As John lay at His feet, completely dumbfounded, this extraordinary figure placed the
same right hand that held seven stars on John saying, 'Do not
be afraid. I am the First and the Last. I am the Living One; I was
dead, and behold I am alive for ever and ever!'[8] That day John
encountered the Lord God Almighty, Jesus Christ.

As the vision unfolds, John journeys to the throne in
heaven, the Holy of Holies. Here we are privileged to catch a
glimpse of the worship of heaven:

> In the centre, around the throne, were four living creatures, and
> they were covered with eyes, in front and in back. The first living
> creature was like a lion, the second was like an ox, the third had
> a face like a man, the fourth was like a flying eagle. Each of the
> four living creatures had six wings and was covered with eyes all
> around, even under his wings. Day and night they never stop say-
> ing: "Holy, holy, holy is the Lord God Almighty, who was, and is,
> and is to come." Whenever the living creatures give glory, honour
> and thanks to him who sits on the throne and who lives for ever
> and ever, the twenty-four elders fall down before him who sits on
> the throne, and worship him who lives for ever and ever. They lay
> their crowns before the throne and say: "You are worthy, our Lord
> and God, to receive glory and honour and power, for you created
> all things, and by your will they were created and have their
> being."[9]

---

[8] Revelation 1:17–18
[9] Revelation 4:6–11

What an incredible sight these four living creatures must have been. Covered in eyes, in front and in back. I have often wondered why they have so many eyes. Perhaps it is in order to better see and take in the wonder of God. As they catch sight of the One seated on the throne they cry, 'Holy, holy, holy is the Lord God Almighty, who was, and is, and is to come.' Day and night they never stop saying it. Even now as you read through these words, they are at it. 'Holy, holy, holy...' Tonight, when your head hits the pillow and you fall asleep, they will continue, 'Holy, holy, holy. . .' I sometimes imagine them beginning to flag; I mean it must get pretty exhausting! As they tire they catch another glimpse of the great I AM and their hearts soar with praise, 'Holy, holy, holy. . .' Every fresh revelation, every different angle, every moment of insight fuels the praise of heaven.

As all this goes on, the 24 elders join in. While the living creatures give glory and honour and thanks, the 24 elders fall down before Him who sits on the throne and worship. They cast their crowns before such greatness and say, 'You are worthy, our Lord and God, to receive glory and honour and power, for you created all things, and by your will they were created and have their being.' This perpetual worship goes on all around us. It never stops. The heavens never become exhausted of worshipping. It doesn't become monotonous or predictable. It simply goes on and on and on.

Just think about that for a moment. The God we worship is so unbelievably astounding, resplendent, powerful and majestic, that for all of eternity we will never grow weary of worshipping Him. It is interesting to note this journey of worship in Revelation. They recognise and then respond. As they get caught up in responding and pouring out praise, they recognise more. As they recognise more, they respond with even greater vigour and passion. The process of recognising and responding never ends; it is eternal worship. One day we too will be drawn up to join the hosts of heaven praising forever. For now we see in part, but one day we will see face to face. What a glorious day!

Eyes of mercy

God reveals Himself as all-powerful and holy, but He also discloses himself as merciful and kind. One of my favourite 'Jesus' stories in the Bible is the one about the woman caught in adultery. I can picture the scene. This probably half-naked and utterly terrified woman is literally dragged by the religious leaders through the town and into the Temple where Jesus is standing. She has been caught red-handed having sex with a man who is not her husband. At that time this was seen as one of the worst things that a woman could do, and the punishment was death by stoning.

The woman has probably already taken a few hits and knows very well what is coming next. But every one of those leaders has their eyes fixed on Jesus, waiting to see what He will do. They probably have their stones in their hands and are ready to kill. But in that moment Jesus does something totally unexpected. He thinks for a moment, and then turns to the leaders and says, 'If any one of you is without sin, let him be the first to throw a stone at her.'[10] I bet you could have cut the atmosphere with a knife: the woman stands there shaking with fear, the leaders don't know what to do next, and all the

---

[10] John 8:7

while Jesus waits, strong and just. One by one they drop their charges and walk away. And then Jesus looks straight into the woman's eyes, and asks her if anyone finds her guilty. She replies, 'No', and Jesus says, 'Then neither do I condemn you. Go now and leave your life of sin.'[11]

The woman expected to find judgement but instead, in the eyes of Jesus, she found mercy. As she encountered the kindness of God, she was moved to repentance. From that day on, she was never the same again.

All-consuming

I was sitting at the back of the church, minding my own business. As I looked out and watched people worshipping I noticed a few enthusiasts at the front waving brightly coloured flags. I remember telling myself that I'd never do anything like that – it was not for me. Then, my heart skipped a beat as I sensed God prompt me to respond to Him in worship by waving a flag. To be honest I laughed it off, thinking it was my mind playing tricks, but gradually I came to a conviction that it was the Lord speaking. I wrestled with these thoughts for a while, pleading with God not to make me do it. All the while we were singing, 'I'll bring you more than a song, for a song in itself is not what you have required'. I knew what I had to do. Leaving my seat I walked to the front, picked up one of the less brightly coloured flags, and started to wave it. I could feel the eyes of all my friends burning in the back of my head. As I waved the flag something inside me died, but my worship came alive. I never want my

---

[11] John 8:11

pride, or fear of man, to get in the way of God-encounters like these.

Worship should be all-consuming. When our eyes are open to see the greatness and the kindness of our God, we should respond with every fibre of our being. As John Piper writes,

> If God's reality is displayed to us in His Word, and we do not then feel in our heart any grief or longing or hope or fear or awe or joy or confidence, then we may dutifully sing and pray and recite and gesture as much as we like, but it will not be real worship. We cannot honour God if our hearts are far from Him. The engagement of the heart in worship is the coming alive of the feelings and emotions and affections of the heart. Where feelings for God are dead, worship is dead.[12]

It should be common in our churches to see people weeping in worship, overwhelmed by the depth of God's mercy. It should be common to see people dancing like lunatics, free and abandoned before their Maker. It should be common to be overcome by the enormous volume of people singing and shouting praise at the tops of their voices. It should be common to see people lost in silence, no one wanting to move, totally transfixed by the transcendence of God. Recently a friend of mine emailed me about a time of worship he had been involved in. He described it, saying it was 'as much of heaven as a human can take without exploding!' What a great definition of worship.

John Stott writes, 'There is something fundamentally flawed about a purely academic interest in God. God is not an appropriate object for cool, critical, detached, scientific

---

[12] John Piper, *Desiring God*, Multnomah, 2003, p.83

observation. No, the true knowledge of God will always lead us to worship . . . our place is on our faces before Him in adoration.'[13]

As we delve into His Word, as we behold His glory spectacularly displayed throughout creation, as we reverently draw near to God, His wonderful promise is that He will draw near to us. Beholding His beauty, we are left forever undone. For to know God is to love God.

---

[13] John Stott, quote taken from www.thequotes.wordpress.com

3

Creation joins as one to sing...

Still your heart. Quiet your soul. Turn the radio off. Step outside and allow yourself to tune in. Can you hear the sound? The wind rushing through the trees, the waves lapping against the shore, the birds filling the air with melody, the cry of a child amidst the roar of traffic? Creation alive in song, responding to its Creator.

St Paul's Cathedral overlooks the City of London and remains one of its most famous and stunning landmarks. The cathedral, completed in 1710, is the work of the architect Sir Christopher Wren. The work and skill of Wren is a true masterpiece. However, search throughout the cathedral and you will find no memorial to its designer. Rather, in its place, there is an inscription over the north door saying, 'If you are looking for a memorial, look around you.' The celebration of Sir Christopher Wren's accomplishments can be found not on a grand plaque or ostentatious statue, but simply through looking at what he has built: the architecture speaks for itself.

Creation surrounds us, full of beauty and wonder, revealing the greatness of its Creator.

The medieval philosopher and theologian Bonaventura put it like this,

> All creatures of this sensible world lead the soul of the wise and contemplative person to the eternal God, since they are the shadows, echoes and pictures, the vestiges, images and manifestations of that most powerful, most wise and best first principle, of that eternal origin, light and fullness, of that productive, exemplary and order-giving Art. They are set before us for the sake of our knowing God, and are divinely given signs. For every creature is by its very nature a kind of portrayal and likeness of that eternal Wisdom.[1]

So often in life we need to take time to stop and consider God's wonders.[2] The universe around us is God's breathtaking masterpiece. Consider the silent beauty of the stars. Human empires rise and fall, yet the star-studded heavens continue to shine, majestic and glorious. Recently I was reading about a collection of stars known as neutron stars. As far as stars go they are actually quite small, often measuring no more than 16 kilometres across. Unbelievably though, one teaspoon of this matter weighs three billion tons. So dense is this matter that if a small piece of neutron star dropped onto the ground it would slice through the earth like a bullet through cotton.

Consider the dimensions of space. We live in a vast universe. If we could travel in a space shuttle at a speed of 50,000 kilometres per hour, it would take over 88,000 years to reach

---

[1] Quoted in *Glimpsing the Face of God*, Alister McGrath, Lion, 2002, p.50
[2] Job 37:14

the star that is nearest to our sun, Proxima Centauri. Incredibly, if the sun were the size of the dot over a letter 'i', the nearest star would be a dot 16 kilometres away.

Consider the oceans, full of varied and spectacular life. A nearly invisible fish swims among the icebergs of Arctic and Antarctic waters. It manages to survive in the freezing waters due to a special protein that acts like an anti-freeze to keep crystals from forming inside its body. With no haemoglobin or red pigment in its blood, it has a ghostly white appearance and almost transparent colouring.

Stretching from between 1,000 to 5,000 metres down, lies the 'Ocean Deep'. Scientists recently exploring these depths have discovered 500 previously unknown species of marine life. These include a furry crab, a squid that can chew its food, and a shrimp that survives alongside volcanic vents that spew out water heated to 470 °C. Scientists believe there are plenty more surprises to discover, with an estimated 90 per cent of marine life in the world as yet undocumented.[3] Alistair Fothergill says, 'We know more about the surface of the moon than the deep oceans of our own planet.'[4]

Consider the Grand Canyon, the largest gorge on planet Earth. Stretching 465 kilometres across the face of the Colorado Plateau in northern Arizona, USA, rim to rim it measures up to 29 kilometres across, with an average width of 16 kilometres and an average depth of 1.6 kilometres. At the canyon's bottom, the Colorado River cuts through Granite Gorge, exposing some of the oldest rocks visible anywhere on

[3] Taken from *The Week*, 'Health and Science' section, Issue 595, 6th January 2007

[4] Andrew Byatt, Alistair Fothergill and Martin Holmes, *The Blue Planet*, BBC Worldwide Ltd, 2001

earth, some nearly two billion years old. John Wesley Powell, an American explorer, once described the sound of rushing water in the canyon as 'a symphony of multitudinous melodies'.[5]

Consider the intricate design of the human body. One human brain generates more electrical impulses in a single day than all the telephones in the world put together. In 2.5 square centimetres of skin there lie 3.6 metres of nerve fibres, 1,300 nerve cells, 100 sweat glands, 3 million cells, and 2.7 metres of blood vessels. The average human heart will beat 3,000 million times in its lifetime and pump 48 million gallons of blood. Amazingly, the human thighbone is stronger than concrete. Whether you feel it or not, our human bodies are exceptional masterpieces, perfectly designed to hold together and perform.

The starlit heavens, the oceans below, the mountain heights, every creature great and small, have all been made for a purpose: to declare the glory of God and proclaim the work of His hands.[6] Day and night they join together to sing this symphony of praise.

Creation's song

The song of creation can be found all throughout the Scriptures. In the book of Job, we see the Lord ask the question of who made the earth's foundations: '. . .who laid its cornerstone – *while the morning stars sang together* and all the angels shouted for joy?'[7] As creation was breathed into being,

---

[5] wonderclub.com

[6] Psalm 19:1   [7] Job 38:7 (my italics)

the stars joined together, singing as one to respond to their Creator.

In the Psalms we read of the seas lifting up their voice.[8] Could it be that every ocean wave that crashes to the shore is a roar of praise offered up to the Maker of all things? Later we catch a powerful image of creation and humankind joining together in worship:

Shout for joy to the LORD, all the earth, burst into jubilant song with music; make music to the LORD with the harp and the sound of singing, with trumpets and the blast of the ram's horn – shout for joy before the LORD, the King. Let the sea resound, and everything in it, the world and all who live in it. Let the rivers clap their hands, let the mountains sing together for joy. . .[9]

What a beautiful image. The music of our harps, trumpets, drums, guitars and voices, joining with the resounding cheer of the seas, mountains and rivers. This song of creation goes on all around us, demonstrating the glory and greatness of our God.

In Isaiah we find these verses:

You will go out in joy and be led forth in peace; the mountains and hills burst into song before you and the trees of the field will clap their hands.[10]

High heavens, sing! God has done it. Deep earth, shout! And you mountains, sing! A forest choir of oaks and pines and cedars! God has redeemed Jacob. God's glory is on display in Israel.[11]

---

[8] Psalm 93:3

[9] Psalm 98:4–8

[10] Isaiah 55:12

[11] Isaiah 44:23 *The Message*

In C. S. Lewis's book *The Magician's Nephew*, we read a beautiful passage where Aslan, the great lion, creates the world through song. This amazing moment of creation is told through the eyes of Digory, one of the boys in the story:

> In the darkness something was happening at last. A voice had begun to sing. It was very far away and Digory found it hard to decide from what direction it was coming. Sometimes it seemed to come from all directions at once. Sometimes he almost thought it was coming out of the earth beneath them. Its lower notes were deep enough to be the voice of the earth herself. There were no words. There was hardly even a tune. But it was, beyond comparison, the most beautiful noise he had ever heard. It was so beautiful he could hardly bear it . . . Then two wonders happened at the same moment. One was that the voice was suddenly joined by other voices; more voices than you could possibly count. They were in harmony with it, but far higher up the scale: cold, tingling, silvery voices. The second wonder was that the blackness overhead, all at once, was blazing with stars. They didn't come out gently one by one, as they do on a summer evening. One moment there had been nothing but darkness; next moment a thousand, thousand points of light leapt out – single stars, constellations, and planets, brighter and bigger than any in our world. There were no clouds. The stars and the new voices began at exactly the same time. If you'd seen and heard it, as Digory did, you would have seemed quite certain that it was the stars themselves which were singing, and it was the First Voice, the deep one, which had made them appear and made them sing.[12]

As we listen to creation's song, we are moved to fall more in love with the Creator. Alister McGrath writes, 'It is part of the

---

[12]C. S. Lewis, *The Magician's Nephew*, HarperCollins, 1955, 2005, p. 61

purpose of the creator that we should hear the music of the cosmos, and, through loving its harmonies, come to love their composer.'[13] Every note, every beat and every sound through-out creation reminds us that there is an infinite God who set the world in motion.

However this song of creation isn't simply restricted to the earth. We see that, in the worship that surrounds the throne of God, creation joins with the chorus of heaven worshipping the Saviour.

> Then I heard every creature in heaven and on earth and under the earth and on the sea, and all that is in them singing: "To him who sits on the throne and to the Lamb be praise and honour and glory and power for ever and ever!"[14]

We have a special role to play in creation's praise. As humans we are called to gather up the praise of creation and put it into words, presenting it before God; as N. T. Wright says, 'To take the inanimate and seemingly inarticulate praise of cre-ation', and give it a voice.[15] We see this in the worship of heaven. As we saw in Chapter 2, the living creatures cry 'Holy, holy, holy is the Lord God Almighty', but it is the 24 elders who can give reason for their praise. They give glory and hon-our because they have minds to understand why God is so worthy. 'You are worthy . . . *for you* created all things, and by your will they were created and have their being.'[16]

Rather than just 'doing worship', as creation does, we

---

[13] Alister McGrath, *Glimpsing the Face of God*, Lion, 2002, p.48

[14] Revelation 5:13

[15] Taken from a Vineyard Equip Interview, titled 'Reclaiming Worship'

[16] Revelation 4:11 (my italics)

humans are given the task of discerning why we should worship. We then have a choice to voice creation's praise or ignore it. Each time we sing, we are enabling creation to praise God. Graham Kendrick and Paul Baloche express this wonderfully in their song 'Creation's King'.

> All creation is a song, waiting to be sung
> All of nature like a prayer, waiting for a tongue
> For who will give it voice
> And make its anthem ring
> Or rise to lead a choir of all created things?
> Lord hear your people sing.[17]

This adds an exciting new dynamic to our congregational times of sung worship. We are speaking and singing on behalf of the whole of creation, joining as one to worship the God who truly is worthy of all praise. When we gather as church we are involved in something so much bigger than simply singing a few worship tunes. We are expressing creation's praise. We are the voice of the trees, the mountains, the oceans, the skies, the whole of creation. The psalmists captures this delightfully:

> Praise him, sun and moon,
> Praise him, all you shining stars. . .
> Praise the LORD from the earth,
> You great sea creatures and all ocean depths,
> Lightning and hail,
> Snow and clouds,

---

[17] Paul Baloche and Graham Kendrick, 'Creation's King', © 2006, Make Way Music (www.grahamkendrick.co.uk) and Integrity's Hosanna! Music/Sovereign Music UK, PO Box 356, Leighton Buzzard LU7 3WP. Used by permission.

Stormy winds that do his bidding,
You mountains and all hills,
Fruit trees and all cedars,
Wild animals and all cattle,
Small creatures and flying birds. . .[18]

We will never run out of songs to sing; we are caught up in an eternal hymn of praise.

If we did not praise

Not everyone can hear creation's praise. Sadly much of the world around us is stuck in a rut, singing the same old boring melodies, tuning in to meaningless songs and sounds. When Jesus made His triumphant entrance into Jerusalem, the whole crowd began joyfully praising God in loud voices saying, 'Blessed is the King who comes in the name of the Lord,' and, 'Peace in heaven and glory in the highest.' Some of the Pharisees in the crowd, riled by this explosion of worship, said to Jesus, 'Teacher, rebuke your disciples!' To this Jesus replied simply, 'I tell you, if they keep quiet, the stones will cry out.'[19] If we do not give voice to the fame of God, then even the stones would cry out and worship; so great is our God.

We as God's creation have a choice. We can sing our own song, write our own tunes, but in the grand scheme of things, compared to creation's symphony, this will only ever amount to a pathetic squeak; a momentary out-of-tune note of little significance. Alternatively we can add our harmonies and

---

[18] Psalm 148:3, 7–10
[19] Luke 19:37–40

melodies to the ceaseless roar of creation, a song so beautiful and haunting that we will never tire of singing along to it. In the quiet of the night I have occasionally tried to listen to the song of the stars. I can tell you, I have never heard them singing about me! I've walked through forests and tried to hear the trees clapping their hands. There has never been a spontaneous rapturous applause to celebrate my presence. However, creation bursts into song celebrating the worth of God. When we choose to join in this song, rightly, we get caught up in something so much bigger than our own individual lives. We get lost in creation's great song, and forever respond to creation's King.

> The rising Sun that fills the sky
> The starry host that lights the night
> Reflecting Your glory
>
> The mountain heights forever stand
> The rain that falls to soak the land
> Respond to Your glory
>
> Almighty God, in every way
> You are above and beyond understanding
> If we did not praise, the rocks would cry out
> Glorious God, high above understanding
>
> The vast expanse of earth and sea
> Held by You in harmony
> Speaks of Your glory
>
> All You've made, since time began
> Life itself; Your perfect plan
> And it's all for Your glory

Creation joins as one to sing
'Glorious God.'
So far above all earthly things.[20]

---

[20] Tim Hughes, 'Almighty God', © 2005 Thankyou Music, tym@kingsway.co.uk. Used by permission.

4

When silence falls...

Have you ever sung this song in church?

> He has driven me away and made me walk in darkness rather than light; indeed, he has turned his hand against me again and again, all day long . . . He has broken my teeth with gravel; he has trampled me in the dust.[1]

Or what about this one?

> How long, O Lord? Will you forget me for ever? How long will you hide your face from me? How long must I wrestle with my thoughts and every day have sorrow in my heart?[2]

I'm guessing that you probably haven't. Most of the churches I've visited in the last few years sing the songs of celebration, joy, praise and adoration, but they seem to miss out the songs of lament. These songs are deemed 'unsuitable' or 'melancholic'. Is it even appropriate to express pain and anger before such a glorious God? I remember hearing one worship leader

---

[1] Lamentations 3:2–3, 16
[2] Psalm 13:1–2

recall that she had just 25 minutes to lead her congregation in worship on a Sunday '. . . so why waste time focusing on the negative?'

In his article, 'The Hidden Hope in Lament', Dan Allender writes, 'Christians seldom sing in the minor key. We fear the sombre; we seem to hold sorrow in low-esteem. We seem predisposed to fear lament as a quick slide into doubt and despair; failing to see that doubt and despair are the dark soil that is necessary to grow confidence and joy.'[3]

For generations, people have chosen to wear their Sunday best to church; a form of respect for the Holy God they worship. Whilst there's something honourable about arriving at church prepared, 'dressed-up' and ready to meet with God, I wonder if this emphasis has diminished a place for bringing and sharing our worst before God? A quick glance through the Psalms and other books in the Bible reveal many songs of pain and lament. Cries of despair and suffering continually offered up to God. The theologian Walter Brueggemann comments,

> Nearly one half of the Psalms are songs of lament and poems of complaint. Something is known to be deeply amiss in Israel's life with God. And Israel is not at all reluctant to voice what is troubling [her]. . .The lament-complaint, perhaps Israel's most characteristic and vigorous mode of faith, introduces us to a 'spirituality of protest.' That is, Israel boldly recognises that all is not right in the world. This is against our easy gentile way of denial, pretending in each other's presence and in the presence of God that 'all is well,' when it is not.[4]

---

[3] Dan Allender, 'The Hidden Hope in Lament', Mars Hill Review, 1, 1994, p.25–38

Searching through the Scriptures, and exploring the countless offerings that men and women throughout generations have poured out before God, begs the question: In today's Church have we lost the place of lament in our worship?

Singing the blues

The world is singing the blues. Our media is awash with images of heart-wrenching pain – tsunamis, earthquakes, suicide bombers, riots, murder and abuse. None of us is immune to pain; everybody hurts. I will never forget hearing the devastating sound of a lady at my church screaming at the news that her daughter had just prematurely lost her twin babies. No words could ever describe the depth of torment uttered in her cries and groans. We can relate because in some way we have all experienced the dark night of the soul, those moments in life when each day seems to be filled with sorrow.

In England depression is rife. The number of prescriptions for anti-depressants has risen from 12 million in 1991 to 24 million in 2001.[5] These statistics are not unique to England. People are hurting and desperate. As a friend recently confided in me, 'Tim, is it me? Or is everything in life really painful?' Tune in to the radio and the songs that fill the airwaves predominantly address issues of despair, depression, heartbreak, insecurity, loss of identity and hopelessness. In

---

[4] Walter Brueggemann, Foreword to *Psalms of Lament*, Ann Weems, Westminster John Knox Press, 1995

[5] Taken from a seminar by Michael Green at High Leigh Songwriters' Consultation, 2004

2003, the number one selling song at Christmas in the UK was 'Mad world' by Michael Andrews and Gary Jules.

> Hide my head I wanna drown my sorrow
> No tomorrow, no tomorrow.

It is revealing that, at a time of supposed joy and festivities, the song that most connected with people was a song of bleak despair.

A few years ago I wrote a song called 'When the tears fall'. It was written at a time when life for me was hard. I had recently experienced the personal pain of a breakdown in a relationship. As well as this, I was acutely aware of the agony some of my family and friends were going through. One Sunday morning, my aunt tragically died very suddenly in front of her whole church congregation. Coming to terms with such a grievous blow and seeing the distress of her family was extremely upsetting. On top of this, some close friends were suffering from the hurt and disappointment of numerous miscarriages.

Before long my heart was filled with questions and doubt. One evening, sitting alone in a hotel room in Canada, feeling very low, I starting pouring out my heart to God. The first line I sang out was, 'I've had questions without answers. I've known sorrow, I have known pain.'[6] Immediately I looked for a response. How do you follow a line like that? Well the answer is, look to Jesus. Everyone on this earth experiences pain, heartache, bereavement and illness. The only difference is that for those who believe Jesus is Lord, we have a Saviour

---

[6] Tim Hughes, 'When the tears fall', © 2003 Thankyou Music, tym@kingsway.co.uk. Used by permission.

we can turn and cling to. 'But there's one thing that I'll cling to. You are faithful, Jesus, You're true.'[7]

As I sang out my pain and doubt, my soul found rest. Looking through the song that was taking shape, I immediately thought that this was a personal song for me. However, the more I pondered, the more I realised that here was a song of worship. The sentiment of the song was just as worshipful as 'Here I am to worship'. There has to be a place for expressing pain in our churches. We need a bigger picture of what worship is. Questioning God doesn't mean we are disobeying Him. Expressing doubt doesn't mean we are lacking faith.

The dictionary definition of 'lament' says: 'To utter grief in outcries; to wail; to mourn; sorrow expressed in cries; a musical composition of like character.' We often see lament as a very negative expression, especially when it comes to our relationship with God. More often than not, lament can be seen as self-pity or even rebellion towards God. This couldn't be further from the truth. The whole journey of lament involves asking questions and searching for answers; we press into the unknown. As Dan Allender says, 'A lament uses the language of pain, anger and confusion and moves us towards God.'[8] There is actually something beautiful and selfless about lamenting. To cry out over our own pain and brokenness reveals a longing for a touch of God.

There also has to be a place to despair over the degradation of the world we live in. Millions die every day of HIV AIDS. Hundreds of thousands of children are abused and defiled,

---

[7] Ibid.

[8] Dan Allender, 'The Hidden Hope in Lament', Mars Hill Review, 1, 1994, p.25–38

fatherless and motherless; left to fend for themselves. Communities are ripped apart by war. Injustice is rife. If this doesn't break our hearts and cause us to lament, then there is something seriously warped about our worship. God's heart breaks for the poor, the widow and the orphan. If we long to be more Christlike then I have no doubt we will find ourselves regularly on our knees, weeping over the suffering that goes on in the world we live in. As we do this, we are drawn closer in to the heart of God.

When the tears fall

Some of my favourite worship stories in the Bible involve lament. There is something incredibly moving about the story of Job. Here we see a man – who in the eyes of the world had everything – reduced to nothing. Job was a man who feared God, who was blameless and upright. He had a beautiful family, owned large amounts of land; he was clearly hugely successful. The Bible says he was the 'greatest man among all the people of the East'. But on one horrendous day everything fell apart for Job. His cattle and livestock were destroyed, and most tragically of all his sons and daughters were killed. Picture the scene: a messenger standing before Job, breaking this catastrophic news. How would you respond? 'At this, Job got up and tore his robe and shaved his head. Then he fell to the ground in worship. . .'[9]

What a response. Heartbroken and confused, Job tore his robe and shaved his head; the customary expression of grief

---

[9] Job 1:20

in those days. He then fell to the ground, surrendered himself to God and worshipped. Job didn't hide his pain before God but rather brought his pain before his Creator as he fell to the ground. In that moment, to offer up praise and worship must have been immensely costly. How precious it must have been to God. It is so easy to sing and praise God when everything is going well. What happens though when we sink to the depths?

One of the fascinating aspects of this story is the reaction of Job's three friends. When these men heard of all the troubles that came upon Job they set out to comfort him.

> When they saw him from a distance, they could hardly recognise him; they began to weep aloud, and they tore their robes and sprinkled dust on their heads. Then they sat on the ground with him for seven days and seven nights. No-one said a word to him, because they saw how great his suffering was.[10]

We are often uncomfortable with silence. I have been in so many situations where people have been offered clichéd responses to the pain they are experiencing. 'God has a reason for it.' 'Don't worry, God will make it all all right.' 'God is pruning you through this situation.' This may be true, but when faced with the harsh reality of sorrow and pain, words are often empty. When Job's friends saw the extent of his pain, they were silenced. What could they possibly say to bring comfort? Silence is a gift from God. At times it expresses all that words fail to do.

My friend Mike Pilavachi and I have often led evenings of lament at different churches. The response at times has been

---

[10] Job 2:12–13

overwhelming. In these evenings we worship through song, we delve into the subject and unpack the Scriptures, and then we allow people to respond. Many flood to the front to acknowledge their doubt and sorrow. Some stand, some kneel, many weep. Then we invite others to come and lay a hand on a shoulder or to simply kneel next to someone. This is not a time for words. This is not a time to try and answer questions. Rather, this is a time to weep with those who weep. These evenings have been intensely moving, amazing, God-centred nights of worship. Through talking to people afterwards, it is clear that for many the opportunity to express their lament has been a lifeline in their relationship with God. For me, it has opened my eyes in a new way to the character and nature of God. Here, rather than hindering our worship, the expression of lament has fuelled it.

Expressing anger and pain to God is actually a beautiful and intimate act. Dan Allender says:

> To sing a lament against God in worship reveals far, far greater trust than to sing a jingle about how happy we are and how much we trust him. That kind of song is much like the smiling salesman who meets you with a 'Hey, how are ya. You're looking good today; how can I help ya.' Lament cuts through insincerity, strips pretence, and reveals the raw nerve of trust that angrily approaches the throne of grace and then kneels in awed, robust wonder.[11]

In our everyday lives, the people that we are most likely to share our deepest fears and hurts with are those we love and

---

[11] Dan Allender, 'The Hidden Hope in Lament', Mars Hill Review, 1, 1994, p.25–38

trust the most. True intimacy can be experienced when we choose to share honestly and vulnerably.

I will praise You

If we return to the songs quoted at the start of this chapter, we see that they don't end where I've left them. There is a journey from complaint and petition to a declaration of praise, a movement from despair to faith. In the book of Lamentations the bitter cry ends with words of hope and trust:

> Yet this I call to mind and therefore I have hope: Because of the LORD's great love we are not consumed, for his compassions never fail. They are new every morning; great is your faithfulness.[12]

In the Psalms the feeling of abandonment and sorrow are responded to by singing:

> But I trust in your unfailing love; my heart rejoices in your salvation. I will sing to the LORD, for he has been good to me.[13]

It is easy to praise when everything is going to plan. It is more of a challenge when everything around us is falling apart. It takes great faith to say to God when life is incredibly hard, 'You are good.' But this is the deal. God is good and is forever worthy of our praise. It is not dependent on our feelings. Day and night, God deserves our highest praise.

Keeping God at the centre of our worship enables us to face life's most difficult trials. I think we will find great comfort and healing in the Church by admitting our questions and

---

[12] Lamentations 3:21–23
[13] Psalm 13:5–6

doubts while choosing to trust and praise God in the midst of them. As we lift our eyes up away from ourselves and fix them on Jesus, our Healer, our Saviour, our Defender, our Provider – then we will find hope and joy. Then we will realise that we always have a song in our hearts to sing.

> I will praise You. I will praise You.
> When the tears fall still I will sing to You.
> I will praise You. Jesus praise You.
> Through the suffering still I will sing.[14]

---

[14] Tim Hughes, 'When the tears fall', © 2003 Thankyou Music, tym@kingsway.co.uk. Used by permission.

5

You'll be the song in my heart...

In 1977, on the eve of the American spacecraft *Voyager 1* and *Voyager 2* being launched into the depths of space, a committee of experts gathered together to answer the following question: 'How could you make an alien inhabitant of a planet belonging to a distant star system understand what it is like to be a human being on the planet earth?'

To everyone's surprise, the experts' answer to this strange question was: music. They devoted 87 and a half minutes of the *Voyager* video-message discs to a selection of 'Earth's greatest hits'. The experts felt that music expressed human feelings better than any other medium known to man. There has never been a society without its own distinctive sound and music to express sadness and pain, as well as joy and elation. Taking a varied selection of the earth's music, a gold-plated copper disc was made, featuring sounds from the Aboriginal songs of Australia, the bamboo flutes of Japan, classical pieces by Beethoven, Bach and Mozart, as well as Chuck Berry screaming out 'Johnny B. Goode'. Built to last for up to

1,000 million years, it certainly is the longest lasting disc ever made![1]

Music is glorious. Did you know that most toilets flush in the key of E flat? Perhaps more fascinating, it has been proven that cows produce more milk when listening to music, and chickens lay more eggs when listening to pop music. So if you love your poached eggs and omelettes, then be thankful for Kylie Minogue! On a more serious note, the historian Thomas Carlyle once said, 'Music is well said to be the speech of angels; in fact nothing among the utterances allowed to man is felt to be so divine. It brings us near to the infinite.'[2]

Music has the capacity to tap into human emotions like nothing else. Beethoven once remarked, 'Music should strike fire from the heart of man and bring tears from the eyes of women.'[3] Imagine a movie without a soundtrack, or a party without a sound system, or a restaurant void of musical atmosphere. Music plays a crucial part in our lives. There have been countless moments in my life – driving alone late at night, sleepless on a plane, at a concert, worshipping at church – where a song has been played that has left me speechless and overwhelmed, reduced to tears or feeling invincible.

Music is mysterious. It can be so hard to define 'great music'. What one person loves, another hates. Maybe this explains why musicians throughout generations have had a disliking for music critics. As someone once remarked, 'Asking a musician what he thinks about critics is like asking a lamp-post how it feels about dogs.'[4]

---

[1] Taken from Reader's Digest, 'Did You Know?', 1997, p.350

[2] Ibid., p.132

[3] Quoted from Paul Sullivan, *Sullivan's Music Trivia*, Sanctuary, 2003, p.132

[4] Ibid., p.57

Music is an undeniably powerful force. Throughout culture and society we can see its influence for both good and bad. We've seen the negative effects of music and the excesses of sex, drugs and rock 'n' roll. We need to be aware: music can harm – it informs our ideals and beliefs and can ultimately manipulate our attitudes and behaviour. We are in danger of undoing any good work of the Spirit in us if we're constantly listening to music that encourages violence, misogyny, greed or other destructive values. *The Week* magazine recently reported a health scare of a condition known as 'glam rock shoulder'. It's a condition caused by partygoers punching the air in time to their favourite songs. According to the article, older people who aren't used to letting their hair down on the dance floor are most at risk of suffering from 'glam rock shoulder'.[5] You have been warned!

While we need to be wise about the music we listen to, I wonder whether at times the Church has become afraid of music; fearful of it being used to manipulate and afraid of it becoming an idol. As a result we've kept some music at arm's length. Consequently, it has sadly been the world that has set the standard for great-sounding music. All too often the Church has been a few years behind the pace, settling for imitating rather than pioneering.

William Booth, founder of the Salvation Army, took songs that were being sung in the pubs and on the streets and set godly lyrics to the well-loved melodies. It was Booth who famously coined the phrase, 'Why should the devil have all the best tunes?'[6]

---

[5] http://news.bbc.co.uk/1/hi/scotland/1080222.stm

[6] Quoted from www.salvationarmy.org.uk

For his Christmas message to *War Cry* readers of 1880, William Booth wrote:

> Secular music, do you say, belongs to the devil? Does it? Well, if it did I would plunder him for it, for he has no right to a single note . . . Every note, and every strain, and every harmony is divine, and belongs to us . . . So consecrate your voice and your instruments. Bring out your comets and harps and organs and flutes and violins and pianos and drums, and everything else that can make melody. Offer them to God, and use them to make all the hearts about you merry before the Lord.[7]

I love the passion and purpose of Booth. As God's people in today's society, music is one of the greatest media we have to communicate and express the gospel message. We are in relationship with the Creator of the universe, the God who designed and breathed music into being. It should be His children that are creating heavenly sounds that mould and shape music. We should be setting the trends. The world should be looking to the Church to discover great-sounding melodies and songs.

Healing sounds

In an interview in *Rolling Stone* magazine, Bono said, 'I always believed that music is a transcendent thing, a healing thing.' Bono is not alone in his views. The great German reformer Martin Luther once said,

> Next to the Word of God, music deserves the highest praise. She is a mistress and governess of those human emotions which

---

[7] Quoted from www.salvationarmy.org.uk

control men or more often overtake them. Whether you wish to comfort the sad, to subdue frivolity, to encourage the despairing, to humble the proud, to calm the passionate or to appease those full of hate ... what more effective means than music could you find?[8]

Is it a revolutionary thought that our songs and sounds can 'comfort the sad' and 'encourage the despairing'? These are the songs that I want to listen to; dare I say it – these are the songs that I want to write.

In 1 Samuel there is an intriguing story where David is called to play music for King Saul.

Now the Spirit of the LORD had departed from Saul, and an evil spirit from the LORD tormented him. Saul's attendants said to him, "See, an evil spirit from God is tormenting you. Let our lord command his servants here to search for someone who can play the harp. He will play when the evil spirit from God comes upon you, and you will feel better." So Saul said to his attendants, "Find someone who plays well and bring him to me." One of the servants answered, "I have seen a son of Jesse of Bethlehem who knows how to play the harp. He is a brave man and a warrior. He speaks well and is a fine-looking man. And the LORD is with him." Then Saul sent messengers to Jesse and said, "Send me your son David, who is with the sheep." So Jesse took a donkey loaded with bread, a skin of wine and a young goat and sent them with his son David to Saul. David came to Saul and entered his service. Saul liked him very much, and David became one of his armour-bearers. Then Saul sent word to Jesse, saying, "Allow David to remain in my service, for I am pleased with him." Whenever the

---

[8] Quoted in *The Story of Christian Music*, Andrew Wilson-Dickson, Lion, 1992, p.60

spirit from God came upon Saul, David would take his harp and play. Then relief would come to Saul; he would feel better, and the evil spirit would leave him.[9]

This remarkable story suggests that God can use music to release people from evil manifestations and bring healing and restoration. In a dark and dangerous situation, David allows his beautiful melodies of worship to rise up and as a result relief and light break in. Can you begin to imagine an army of well-accomplished musical worshippers, dedicated to crafting the very best music, heading out to the pubs and clubs to play music over a broken and hurting world; bringing their worship into the dark places? Dare we believe that God could use our songs to bring healing, hope and restoration?

A sweeter song

There is a song that I would give anything to hear. I've heard faint whispers of it, a glimpse of a lyric here and there. It is the song of our Father singing over His beloved. 'The LORD your God is with you, he is mighty to save. He will take great delight in you, he will quiet you with his love, he will rejoice over you with singing.'[10]

I find it is easy to comprehend the idea of music as a gift for us to use to respond to God's love, but I find it completely unfathomable that God would not only take great delight in us but also rejoice over us with singing. I wonder what that song could possibly sound like – without question, a song like no other.

---

[9] 1 Samuel 16:14–23
[10] Zephaniah 3:17

In C. S. Lewis's *The Magician's Nephew* we see another beautiful example of Aslan the Lion singing life into being.

> The Lion was pacing to and fro about that empty land and singing his new song. It was softer and more lilting than the song by which he had called up the star and the sun; a gentle, rippling music. And as he walked and sang the valley grew green with grass. It spread out from the Lion like a pool. It ran up the sides of the little hills like a wave.[11]

The gentle song of the Father brings life and hope to all. Like the rippling effect of a pebble thrown into a pool, this song spreads out knowing no limits or bounds. One of our challenges is to tune into this song. Like tuning a radio, we need to keep listening and waiting until this melody gets louder and clearer. I believe that it is here that we will find so much of our own personal healing, and experience a greater sense of worth. Not only that, but it is here we will gain a sense of the Father's heart for the prodigals. One of my dreams is to see musicians tune into the Father's song and allow the melody to bring transformation. If we could learn to communicate and express this sound through our guitars, drums, voices, cellos, keyboards, or whatever we play, I truly believe we might begin to see many people saved.

What do these songs sound like? They are raw, authentic, passionate, heart-felt, costly, daring and extravagant; divine, Spirit-breathed moments of creativity that reach out to impact the lives of many. I think of a friend of mine, who doesn't yet know Jesus but tells me of the immense peace she finds every time she listens to a worship CD I gave her. I think of the

---

[11] C. S. Lewis, *The Magician's Nephew*, HarperCollins, 1983, p.64

letter I received from the parents of a girl who breathed her last breath, full of hope, listening to a simple song of worship. I think of different friends of mine, venturing into dingy clubs throughout the country, to play their music, offering a message of love and redemption.

I love the scene in the film *The Color Purple* in which a crowd of 'un-churched' people start flooding into the church as they are led by the powerful sound of the choir worshipping with all their hearts. I remember crying as I watched, longing for the day when we would see people in church overwhelmed by the beauty and wonder of God, drawn to the Father by the sounds the church was making. The moment we realise that the Glorious One whispers our names and sweetly sings over us, we will sing a sweeter song.

In Greek mythology the seductive allure of the Sirens was infamous. Sailors were mysteriously lured to shore by the irresistible sound of their songs. Distracted by what they were hearing, the sailors failed to notice the hidden rocks below the surface of the sea, and as their boats began to sink the Sirens set to work devouring and consuming their human flesh.

The story goes that one day Jason, another infamous character in ancient mythology, was set to sail past the island of the Sirens. Aware of the danger, he ordered the most talented musician, Orpheus, to play the most beautiful and melodious songs as they passed by. Jason and his men were so captivated by the music Orpheus played that no one on the boat was distracted by the dangerous sound of the Sirens. Instead, they were hearing a sweeter song.

We are surrounded by music. It is all around us as we shop, eat, walk, work, relax; we can't escape it. Like the songs of the Sirens, so many sounds and messages lead people astray;

sounds and lyrics that are divisive and destructive. But as the hymn states, 'Hark! How the heavenly anthem drowns all music but its own.'[12] The sound of heaven, the song of redemption and the shout of salvation will one day drown out all other music. Even now, we have an opportunity to sing this most glorious song here on the earth.

Could we endeavour to believe that we could write songs that would transform people's lives? Our responsibility is to give of ourselves to become the best musicians we can be; not so that we can look amazing, but rather so the world can better hear the song of heaven. When we start thinking like this, it changes everything. Every time we practise, every hour we rehearse, every moment we labour over lyrics, our hearts are pleading, 'God, glorify Your name. Use us, Lord, to express Your heart and to communicate the sound of heaven.' It quickly becomes so much more than music and songs – it is about the kingdom of God here on the earth.

Behind the music

Music should excite us. It is a God-given gift to be enjoyed. In the book of Revelation, a sign of God's punishment in the fall of Babylon is that 'the music of harpists and musicians, flute players and trumpeters, will never be heard in you again'.[13] God created music, and every day He sings it over us. As we've seen, creation is exploding in song. We have a choice, though, to worship music, or to worship God. If we want to see 'God songs' being played on the radio and being listened to in the

---

[12] M. Bridges, 'Crown Him with many crowns', 1851

[13] Revelation 18:22

clubs, then our highest priority must be God. Before we look to the music, we must look to Him. We can't create these songs in our own strength; it is a spiritual activity. We want people to be left with the fragrance of Jesus. We want their hearts to be tugged by the Holy Spirit. We want their lives to be overwhelmed by the love of the Father.

There was a tremendous celebration when Solomon completed the Temple, and the Ark of the Covenant was set in place. All the priests and musicians were gathered for this historic occasion.

> All the Levites who were musicians – Asaph, Heman, Jeduthun and their sons and relatives – stood on the east side of the altar, dressed in fine linen and playing cymbals, harps and lyres. They were accompanied by 120 priests sounding trumpets. The trumpeters and singers joined in unison, as with one voice, to give praise and thanks to the LORD. Accompanied by trumpets, cymbals and other instruments, they raised their voices in praise to the LORD and sang: "He is good; his love endures for ever." Then the temple of the LORD was filled with a cloud, and the priests could not perform their service because of the cloud, for the glory of the LORD filled the temple of God.[14]

The Levites playing cymbals, harps and lyres, 120 priests on trumpets, and the singers joining in with one voice. What a sound! However, I wonder what it was that, over time, people remembered from that day? As impressive as that sound must have been, I speculate that their lasting memory was their extraordinary encounter with God as the Temple was filled majestically with His glory.

---

[14] 2 Chronicles 5:12–14

It is the God behind the music we must seek. Let us love music and embrace the glorious gift that it is – let us join with creation praising God in song. Let us tune into the sound of heaven in the hope that our music might lead others to God. But above all, let us pursue the Giver of music, the God who rejoices over us with singing. 'Come Thou fount of every blessing, tune my heart to sing Your praise.'[15]

---

[15] R. Robinson, 'Come Thou fount of every blessing', 1758

6

I am Yours, Jesus You are mine...

In June 2005, my wife Rachel and I headed off to Tanzania, to spend a week visiting some development projects with the charity Tearfund. We weren't sure what to expect, but we instantly loved it. The warmth of the people, the beauty of the surroundings and the buzz of activity all around us got under our skin. It was, however, a bittersweet experience. Through the smiles, singing and dancing there was death, disease, sorrow, injustice, poverty and extreme hunger. One moment we were laughing, the next we were at a total loss for words.

On our visit we had the opportunity to meet some incredible people. One lady, whose smile will stay with us forever, was Joyce Mbwilo. Living in a village called Uhambingeto, Joyce told us her story of life and survival. With no clean accessible water in the village, she would leave each night at midnight with an empty container. Joyce would then often have to walk for over ten hours until she returned home at

10 a.m. the following morning with water for her family, totally exhausted.

It was estimated that Joyce had walked the equivalent of three times around the world in the pursuit of water. The injustice of this situation was overwhelming, and thankfully through Tearfund's work with local churches there, significant steps are being made to improve life for the people in that village and many others like them. But how could that still be possible in a world today where so many of us have so much? I was deeply struck by the courage and steely determination of Joyce. Lying down and giving up was never an option. Driven by love for her family and an acute awareness of the necessity of clean water for survival, Joyce went to extreme measures to keep her family alive.

In my surroundings, when it comes to survival, I 'want' for nothing. Water is accessible at the turn of a tap. I have food in the fridge and a car in the driveway. There are few things in life that I find myself urgently pursuing.

> O God, you are my God, earnestly I seek you; my soul thirsts for you, my body longs for you, in a dry and weary land where there is no water . . . Because your love is better than life, my lips will glorify you. [1]

> My soul yearns, even faints, for the courts of the LORD; my heart and my flesh cry out for the living God.[2]

These verses from the Psalms express an aching and longing that is often sadly lacking in my life. The object of King David's desire is clearly the Lord. More than life, more than anything

---

[1] Psalm 63:1, 3

[2] Psalm 84:2

else the world could ever offer, David wanted to see and know God. In Jesus we find living water that will satisfy our deepest thirst. This alone should inspire us to pursue more of Him. No matter the cost, no matter how long it takes or how far we have to go to get there, we need to chase after God. As Joyce walked through the night for decades to find water, are we willing to give all we have in order to discover something more important than even water – life itself?

A passionate love affair

The happiest day of my life, without doubt, was when I married the woman of my dreams. All my favourite people gathered together to celebrate our marriage; it was a perfect day. Since then Rachel and I have learned what it means to live together and share life. It's been quite a steep learning curve! I have two younger brothers and grew up in a very 'male' house. As a result women have always been something of a mystery to me. Over recent years I have learned many things about the female psyche but one key discovery (and this is a generalisation, but generalisations are generally true!) is that women need to be cherished. They need to be wooed, romanced and adored.

Often Rachel will say to me, 'Tim, you haven't said how beautiful I am today.' To this I want to reply by saying, 'But Rachel, I told you how beautiful you were last week! Can't we have an agreement that unless I say otherwise, you should assume that I think you are beautiful?' Marriage counsellors, fear not – I didn't actually say it! Perhaps my biggest mistake in our relationship was when we were dating. We had reached the stage in our relationship where we were beginning to talk about marriage. One afternoon we were talking together and Rachel shared how much she loved me and said that she knew beyond a shadow of doubt that I was the one for her. I wanted to say something equally romantic back to her in response, but all I could hear coming out of my mouth was, 'Rachel, I'm 99 per cent sure as well.' Apparently 99 per cent isn't good enough!

In order to have a healthy relationship with my wife, I need to take time to be intimate with her and to express my love for her. If I don't, then pretty soon our relationship will turn sour. It is the same with God: if we are not drawing close to Him and seeking His face, then our relationship suffers. To keep the flame alive we need to keep making an effort to adore Him. So simple, yet sadly too often we get distracted. We are too busy, overworked, stressed and overwhelmed; we don't take time out to be still and know that He is God.

G. K. Chesterton wrote, 'Sometimes our religion is more a theory than a love affair.' We need to find time to be intimate with our Saviour, to respond to His mercy and enjoy Him forever.

We were made for intimacy; to be known and to know. When deprived of intimacy we suffer. There is a vacuum within us that craves to be loved and accepted for who we are.

In 1996, the US Masters golf championships took place at Augusta. Being one of the most prestigious of golfing contests, a lot was at stake. On the final day, Greg Norman and Nick Faldo went head to head. With a six-shot lead, the championship appeared to have Norman's name written all over it, but all did not go according to plan. In only a short amount of time, unbelievably, the tables had turned, and on the eighteenth green, an ashen-faced Norman watched Nick Faldo sink a putt that won him the coveted 'Green Jacket' and crowned him the US Masters champion. In a sporting gesture, Faldo embraced Norman, and to the great shock of millions of viewers Norman broke down in tears. Afterwards, at the press conference, Greg Norman was pressed to explain the reason for his breakdown. He told them that as a child his father had not shown him any warmth or affection and would only ever shake his hand. When Nick Faldo hugged him, he realised that it was the first time he had been hugged as a grown man. In that moment something inside of him broke.

The secret of success

We live in a society that drives us towards success. We all know a sense of pressure to succeed and make something of our lives. Our culture places pressure on us to get high exam results, get into the right university, get a great job, earn lots of money, get married, have the perfect family, own a home, and make our lives count for something. At every stage in life it feels like there is a pressure to succeed. Pressure, pressure, pressure. And this pressure to be successful can drive us into the ground.

A while ago the *Daily Telegraph* ran an article entitled, 'How the pressure to succeed is creating a generation of unruly, depressed teenagers.' In the article it stated that the number of 15-year-olds suffering from anxiety and depression has increased by 70 per cent since the mid 1980s.[3]

Even worse, we are seeing the rate of teenage suicides grow as the years go by. I was devastated to hear of an old

---

[3] Article by Sarah Womack, posted 14/09/2004, www.telegraph.co.uk/news/main

school friend of mine who committed suicide at university. I remember how stressed he would get when exam time came around. His parents were desperate for him to succeed and he was anxious to live up to their expectations. At university his studies did not go as well as he had hoped. Having failed his exams he concealed the truth from his parents, dreading their disappointment. After months of deception, it all became too much.

But success is not only measured by our achievements. Success is about our need to be accepted, our need to be loved. Driven by this need we push ourselves to try and earn respect and gain acceptance. We work crazy hours to achieve promotion. We push our bodies to the limits to make the grade. But is it ever enough? As Freddie Mercury, the lead singer of Queen, wrote,

> 'You can have everything in the world and still be the loneliest man, and that is the most bitter type of loneliness. Success has brought me world idolisation and millions of pounds, but it's prevented me from having the one true thing we all need – a loving, ongoing relationship.'[4]

I recognise in my own life a need for acceptance and significance. I frequently feel the pressure to succeed as a husband, worship leader, songwriter, friend, even as a Christian. Ultimately the desire to be loved is not a purely misguided perception. Nor are our hopes and dreams wrong in themselves. However, for me sometimes my desire for success becomes an unhealthy distraction; a warped sense of trying to continually earn something that is beyond me. It leaves me exhausted and

---

[4] http://www.queenarchives.com/viewtopic.php?t=168

frustrated. If only I could write that song. If only I could achieve that goal.

The wonderful truth about our God is that He loves us more than we could ever begin to comprehend. Recently a friend shared this phrase with me and it has stuck in my head, challenging, inspiring and reforming me: 'I am loved by God, and I love God, therefore I am successful.' Allow these words to sink into your heart. Perhaps this is the antidote to society's pressure to achieve. Could this simple truth be the real secret of success?

Regardless of who we are and what we have done, God has made it plain that He loves us unconditionally. No achievement in life could ever top that. There is nothing in this world that could bring us greater happiness or fulfilment. It all starts with us receiving God's unfailing love. As in Michelangelo's painting on the Sistine Chapel ceiling, God reaches down to touch each one of us. 'We love because he first loved us.'[5] We tend to try and earn love, but here God makes it clear that first and foremost we must receive His love. It is a gift to us, freely given.

When my nephew Noah was born I went to visit him and his parents in hospital. There he was sleeping away totally oblivious to the pain and stress he had caused his mum and dad, particularly his mum! The labour had lasted over 36 hours. Not only that but, with having to be fed regularly, Noah was keeping his parents up through most of the night. If all that wasn't enough, Noah had cost his parents a small fortune: buggies, nappies, clothes, car seats, a newly decorated nursery. With Noah it was one-way traffic. Take, take, take. There was no, 'Thanks Mum and Dad for bringing me into this

---

[5] 1 John 4:19

world.' Not even a smile to say thank you. How ungrateful! But looking at his mum and dad, you could see that they totally adored him. They loved him with all their hearts; in a moment he had become their pride and joy. Noah did not have to earn his parents' love. They loved him because he was theirs. We could learn a lesson or two from Noah and his parents.

In Matthew's Gospel, we see the amazing moment when Jesus was baptised by John. As soon as Jesus was baptised the heavens opened and a voice declared, 'This is my Son, whom I love; with him I am well pleased.'[6] Before Jesus had started his ministry, before he had performed any great miracles, before He had healed anyone, before He had raised anyone from the dead, His father was pleased with Him.

If we want to be a people who impact this world, then here is a crucial truth: We must learn to be loved by God. We need to learn to accept the free gift of God's love; to accept that it cannot be earned, that it is not distributed according to our success. We need to embrace Him and learn to enjoy all that He has showered upon us. As this truth becomes the rock on which we build our lives, we can boldly step out, knowing that 'if God is for us, who can be against us?'[7]

In King David we see this assured boldness. For all his mistakes and failures, of which there were many, he had an unshakeable understanding of God's unceasing love for him. Reading through some of the psalms it's quite startling.

In Psalm 17:8, David prays, 'Keep me as the apple of your eye.' Refreshing to see that David already assumed and believed that he was the apple of God's eye. In Psalm 18:19 he declares, 'He brought me out into a spacious place; he

---

[6] Matthew 3:17   [7] Romans 8:31

rescued me because he delighted in me.' Incredible to see such boldness and confidence in God's heart of love. In Psalm 41:11, David says to God, 'I know that you are pleased with me.' How many of us could say that with confidence before God? Psalm 139:13–16 contains these famous words:

> For You created my inmost being; you knit me together in my mother's womb. I praise you because I am fearfully and wonderfully made; your works are wonderful, I know that full well. My frame was not hidden from you when I was made in the secret place. When I was woven together in the depths of the earth, your eyes saw my unformed body.

It is imperative that we grasp what David knew to be true: that we are loved and adored.

David lived in the certainty that he was loved by God. For David this was the pinnacle of success. In moments of sinfulness he would stand before God and say, 'Here I am God. I've messed up again, but *I know You love me*.' Or when he was full of doubt and fear, he could say, 'God where are You? Why have You deserted me? Don't let me go because *I know You love me*.' Free and abandoned before his King, with childlike faith David boldly approached God's throne and courageously lived out his beliefs. David was a passionate and extravagant worshipper who found meaning and contentment in the eyes of His Father. These verses suggest that David did not link his earthly success, or lack of it, with his acceptance of God's love. We too need to journey towards the realisation that God's love for us is constant, in spite of the things we do.

I remember on one particular occasion being profoundly challenged about my perception of God's love for me. A top London banker, who happened to be a Christian, called me one day and invited me for lunch. As we ate, he hesitantly mentioned that he felt he had an encouragement for me. He felt God had given him a picture of me kneeling down before the Lord, singing to Him these words from the song, 'Here I am to worship':

> You're altogether lovely,
> Altogether worthy,
> Altogether wonderful to me.[7]

Then he saw the Lord sing those same words over me. Initially I found this really hard to accept; surely God couldn't sing that over me. But the stunning truth is that God does indeed delight in us and rejoice over us with singing. I left that lunch meeting overcome with the depth of God's love for me.

All of me

So how do we respond to this love? By giving all that we are in response. The former Vicar of Holy Trinity Brompton, Bishop Sandy Millar, tells the story of attending a church conference. Having been inspired by all that was going on, he went for a walk along the beach. Pouring his heart out to God he was so thankful for all that was going on in the life of Holy Trinity. As he prayed, he suggested things that he could offer up for God to use. Asking the question, 'God what do You want from me?', he felt God clearly say, 'Sandy, all I want is you.' Before we get caught up making grand statements and trying to offer up to God our money, achievements and ambitions, we need to first and foremost offer up ourselves. All that we are, all that we have, and all that we will ever be.

---

[2] Tim Hughes, 'Light of the world', © 2000 Thankyou music, tym@kingsway.co.uk. Used by permission.

7

Living for Your glory...

Daily our senses are bombarded with the message that we are the most important thing on the face of the earth. 'Buy this, you're worth it.' 'Treat yourself, you deserve it.' Recently I read the story of a business tycoon dubbed as 'Britain's vainest man'. He has spent £55,000 on a new set of teeth and twice daily injects himself with growth hormones at an annual cost of £10,000. On top of this, he has dedicated one wall of his penthouse to a £10,000 portrait of himself. And if that wasn't enough, the 31-year-old has spent £3 million on an entire Bulgarian coastal town, which he has renamed after himself.[1]

We are led to believe that the world revolves around us. As one advertising slogan says, 'It's all about you.' However, a brief flick through the Scriptures, or a walk through spectacular scenery, quickly raises the question: Is there something bigger and greater than us? The world does revolve around

---

[1] *The Week*, Issue 566, 10th June 2006, p.14

someone, but it isn't you and it certainly isn't me. So, whose name are we living for? Are we living to make God famous or to make ourselves famous?

Whose name are we living for?

From generation to generation, the story of David and Goliath has been told and retold with relish and excitement. On one hill, the Philistine army assembled, prepared and ready for war. On another hill, under Saul's command, the Israelite army gathered. At regular intervals the towering figure of the Philistine warrior Goliath would scream and shout threats and abuse to the Israelite army. The gauntlet had been laid down. Send a man from the Israelite ranks to fight Goliath. If he overcame and killed the nine-foot giant then the Philistines would become subject to the Israelites. If Goliath was victorious then it was game over for Israel. For 40 days, every morning and every evening, Goliath took his stand, terrifying and dismaying the Israelite army. Amongst the most fearsome and trained warriors of Israel, not one was willing to take on his challenge. That is until David, son of Jesse, a young shepherd boy, overheard Goliath's fearsome rant. David, angered by Goliath's torrent of abuse, and appalled that he should defy the 'army of the living God', boldly declared, 'Let no one lose heart on account of this Philistine; your servant will go and fight him.' There must have been a ripple of laughter among the Israelite army. What chance would David have? It was absurd.

We know the story. David, after persuading Saul, stepped out armed with a sling and five smooth stones. With one shot, the stone crashed into Goliath's forehead, knocking him dead.

David had conquered; he was victorious. Against the odds, Israel had a new hero.

Reading through the story, there is an amazing truth. At no point before stepping out to fight does David mention his own name. Twice when speaking to King Saul he refers to himself simply as 'your servant'.

> '. . .your servant will go and fight him.'[2]

> '. . .your servant has been keeping his father's sheep.'[3]

Only after David had slain Goliath, did Saul turn to the commander of the army and ask,

> 'Abner, whose son is that young man?'
> Abner replied, 'As surely as you live, O king, I don't know.'[4]

How amazing! David had achieved the unthinkable, and no one had a clue who he was. If I had been in David's shoes I would have made sure that everyone was aware of my name. I would have played the 'martyr card'. 'My name is Tim Hughes. If I die heroically and people want to honour me by building a statue, then please take my correct measurements. I'm 6 feet tall. If possible could you include a six-pack in any sculptures.' I would have wanted to go out in a blaze of glory. Not so for David. He was not bothered about his own press. He was focused and determined on directing all eyes to the God he so passionately loved and worshipped.

In the film *Amadeus* the life story of Wolfgang Amadeus

---

[2] 1 Samuel 17:32

[3] 1 Samuel 17:34

[4] 1 Samuel 17:55

Mozart is told through the eyes of fellow composer Antonio Salieri. As court composer to Emperor Joseph II, Salieri was a highly gifted composer. However, wracked with jealousy and bitterness, he lived his life despising the astonishing natural gift and skill of Mozart. During the film there is a telling scene in which a young Salieri, alone in church, prays to God, 'Lord make me a great composer. Let me celebrate your glory through music and be celebrated myself. Make me famous through the world, dear God. Make me immortal.'

How often in the quietness of our hearts do we recite a similar prayer? There are sentiments in Salieri's prayer that are honourable and upright; aspects that we would do well to pray ourselves: 'Lord make me a great composer.' In all that we do we need to pray for God's inspiration to enable us to be the best that we can be. This is not in itself a selfish prayer. The prayer continues, 'Let me celebrate Your glory through music . . .' Again, we need to seek to celebrate God's glory through whatever we do, be it teaching, art, film, law, medicine, design, etc. What a wonderful prayer that God's glory would be demonstrated and enjoyed as we excel in our God-given gifts. However, it's here that the prayer turns inward and sour: '. . . and be celebrated myself. Make me famous through the world, dear God. Make me immortal.' For Salieri this is the catch. The real desire of his heart was that he would be recognised and adored.

Sadly, I sometimes find myself praying a similar prayer: 'God I want these songs to bring glory and fame to You, but please may I become successful through them as well.' Or perhaps another prayer that is dressed up in spiritual language and more subtle: 'Lord allow me to minister on a bigger platform so that many more people will come to know and worship You.' It almost sounds honourable. Surely that is a good thing, that many people come to know and love God. But so often that is not our highest aim. Like Salieri I crave the praise of man. The stark reality is that this prayer reveals the pride and arrogance that darkens my heart. Am I really passionate about God's renown – or my own? Would I be equally passionate about leading worship and writing songs if I only ever led before a small group of people?

There is a verse that appears twice in Luke's Gospel: 'For everyone who exalts himself will be humbled, and he who humbles himself with be exalted.'[5]

It is interesting to note that this verse is based around active verbs. I used to think that humility was a gift that floated down from heaven into our laps. A person was either full of humility or full of pride. It was a personality trait that people were born with. Now my understanding has completely shifted. There is a responsibility for us to seek after humility, actively choosing to humble ourselves before a glorious God.

I still have the Bible from my teenage years. Inscribed on the opening page is a heartcry that I continue to pray. 'I want to be a humble, passionate servant.' If we don't passionately endeavour to pursue humility, to live for God's name, then we start living for our own name. We start exalting ourselves. That is why everyday we must chase after humility.

A while back, after a Sunday evening service, I was chatting to my keyboard player. A visitor to our church came up and asked me if I remembered the fourth or fifth song we had sung that night. I started going through song titles. 'Was it

---

[5] Luke 14:11; Luke 18:14

'Open the eyes of my heart'?' 'No.' 'What about 'Give thanks to the Lord'?' 'No.' And then it dawned on me – perhaps she meant my song, 'Here I am to worship'. Expecting her to share the story of how she had been profoundly impacted by this song I continued, 'Is it the song, 'Here I am to worship. Here I am to bow down'?' I even gently sang the chorus to trigger her memory! I stood back, waiting to have my ego stroked. However, she replied, 'Oh no I hate that song. People at my church sing that song and whenever I hear it I want to vomit!' They were her exact words. My keyboard player was laughing so hard he fell to the floor. I quickly moved on, hoping she wouldn't discover that I had written the song.

As I reflected on her *outrageous* words, God reminded me of the verse, 'For everyone who exalts himself will be humbled, and he who humbles himself with be exalted.' I had got carried away; I had started to think I was something special. In that moment God graciously reminded me that I'm just a guy who writes songs that make people want to vomit! It was a timely reminder.

The Bible is clear: if we don't choose to bow down reverently before God, then we will be humbled. He is God. We are not. He seems to prefer it that way. God's Word through Isaiah is a powerful reminder to us.

> The LORD Almighty has a day in store for all the proud and lofty, for all that is exalted (and they will be humbled) . . . The arrogance of man will be brought low and the pride of men humbled; the LORD alone will be exalted in that day, and idols will totally disappear . . . In that day men will throw away to the rodents and bats their idols of silver and idols of gold, which they make to worship. They will flee to caverns in the rocks and to overhanging crags from dread of the LORD and the splendour of his majesty,

when he rises to shake the earth. Stop trusting in man, who has but a breath in his nostrils. Of what account is he?[6]

So how can we actively cultivate and develop a heart of humility?

Consider the vastness of God

On 20th August 1977, *Voyager II*, the interplanetary probe launched to observe and transmit to Earth data about the outer planetary system, set off from Earth travelling faster than the speed of a bullet. On 28th August 1989 it reached planet Neptune, 4,345 million kilometres from Earth. *Voyager II* then left the solar system. It will not come within one light year of any star for 958,000 years. In our galaxy there are 100,000 million stars like our sun. Our galaxy is one of 100,000 million galaxies.

In a throwaway line in Genesis, the writer tells us, 'He also made the stars.'[7] If you struggled to take all that in then read it again. How great is our God? The universe we live in is vast. As we look up and consider the enormity of our God, we gain perspective. We learn to embrace the smallness of who we are.

Psalm 8 puts it beautifully:

O LORD, our Lord, how majestic is your name in all the earth! You have set your glory above the heavens. From the lips of children and infants you have ordained praise because of your enemies, to silence the foe and the avenger. When I consider your heavens,

---

[6] Isaiah 2:12, 17–18, 20–22

[7] Genesis 1:16

the work of your fingers, the moon and the stars, which you have set in place, what is man that you are mindful of him, the son of man that you care for him?[8]

We are 'but a breath' in comparison to Almighty God. The more we ponder and dwell upon the glory of God, the more we put into perspective who we are.

Invest in obscurity

I love to serve. When there are lots of onlookers then I am amazing at doing the washing up, setting out chairs, even hoovering. However, take the crowd away, and I become reluctant to do any of those behind-the-scenes chores. I believe that a key way to cultivate a humble heart is to learn the art of servanthood.

I was struck by the story of a well-known American worship leader. Feeling a call by God to lead worship, he approached his pastor to tell him of his availability to lead the worship at the church. His pastor graciously informed him that there was no position available at that time for a 'worship leader', but that they were looking for a janitor. Thinking this would be a short-term post before stepping up to become the worship leader, this guy took on the job. For weeks and then months, he spent his days stacking chairs, cleaning toilets and locking up last thing at night. As time went on he became more and more bitter and frustrated. Why was he wasting his time on menial tasks that anyone could do? But one morning, whilst mopping the floor, he suddenly had a revelation that what he was doing was worship. Every chair stacked, every light bulb

---

[8] Psalm 8:1–4

repaired, every kind deed done to help others, if done to the glory of God, was a precious offering of worship. It was here that he learnt the heart of worship.

God is looking for servants, not stars. In what ways are you choosing to serve those around you? How are you investing in obscurity by doing those jobs that no one sees or can give you credit for? As we do these things, I have no doubt that we will grow in humility.

Choose to prefer others

Jealousy is an ugly trait. It is so sad to see people consumed by jealousy and resentment. At times it can be really hard to see our friends thrive and prosper when it feels like we are not. By putting others first and by choosing to rejoice in others' successes, we are choosing to humble ourselves.

Recently I was involved in a worship conference in Australia. Throughout the week most of the worship was wonderfully led by Darlene Zschech. One afternoon I was down to lead with two other worship leaders from her team. We ran through a few songs and were prepared to lead. About ten minutes before the meeting Darlene turned up. The two guys went straight up to her and were saying, 'Darlene you lead. It's so great when you lead it. We'll back you up.' She replied saying, 'No, no – you guys lead. It will be so amazing if you lead it.' I stood back watching as they argued amongst themselves, each trying to persuade the other to lead. I wanted to step in and say, 'Guys, I'll lead!'

What a model of a team preferring one another. There was such a strong sense of community and life in that place. There were no egos. It was a group of people passionate about drawing all the attention to God. I have no doubt that the humility of those involved has been formed and shaped by their desire to prefer one another. If you often find yourself thinking, 'I should be leading there', 'I'm more gifted than her', 'I write better songs than him', then choose to prefer others. Bless those that you struggle with. Talk highly of those that you feel envious of. It will lead to humility.

In the eighteenth century, two theologians, George Whitefield and John Wesley, were well documented for having strong and differing theological opinions. One day someone asked Whitefield the brave question, 'Will you see John Wesley in heaven?' To this Whitefield responded, 'I fear not.' As the crowd gasped in shock, he continued, 'He will be so near the throne and me at such a distance that I shall hardly get a sight of him.'

This is exactly the attitude we need to develop. We might not agree with everyone or even connect with all people, but wouldn't it be amazing if we could learn to prefer one another? Can you begin to imagine the impact of a church united and choosing to honour and support one another? When Ronald Reagan was President of the United States, he had a sign on his desk saying, 'There is no limit to how far a person can go as long as he doesn't care who gets the credit.'

We can get so preoccupied about who gets praised and credited that an unhealthy competitive streak rises to the surface. Let us remind ourselves of the big picture. To the church in Corinth, who were getting obsessed with names and ministries, Paul wrote,

What, after all, is Apollos? And what is Paul? Only servants, through whom you came to believe . . . I planted the seed,

Apollos watered it, but God made it grow. So neither he who plants nor he who waters is anything, but only God, who makes things grow.[9]

We need to hear and receive these words today. As we learn to prefer one another, we inwardly cultivate a humble heart. No longer are we consumed with our own personal gain. Rather we long to see God's kingdom come, and for His name to be lifted high above all other names – including our own.

---

[9] 1 Corinthians 3:5–7

8

Christ in me the hope of glory...

A few years ago I met a retired Anglican bishop from South
Africa. As we talked he told me about his retirement
plans. He had been unsure for months as to what the future
would hold, but he kept on praying, 'Lord show me what it is
that I can do, that You will bless.' For months he prayed this
prayer but felt God was silent. After a while he realised that
all this time he had been praying the wrong prayer. He felt
God tell him that what he needed to pray was, 'Lord what is
it that You are doing that I can bless?' The two prayers seem
so similar, but they are significantly different.

Our journey as worshippers should always be to find out
what pleases the Lord (Ephesians 5:10). In essence, to find out
what God is blessing and get involved with that. Rather than
a 'me-centred' faith, we need to pursue a 'Him-centred' faith.
At the heart of worship, we as God's creation choose to centre ourselves around Him, our Creator. We live to bless Him.

When I read the Bible, one thing seems abundantly clear:
God is passionate about the poor. Jesus made that so apparent,

'The Spirit of the Lord is on me, because he has anointed me to preach good news to the poor' (Luke 4:18). In Amos 5, God's heart burns with anger as He rebukes a people who offer up songs of worship and other choice offerings, but trample and deprive the poor for their own selfish gain. We can't escape the truth – God's heart breaks for the last, least and the lost. If I want to glorify God in all that I do, then issues of justice and poverty need to be at the core of who I am.

Speaking at the US National Prayer Breakfast in 2006, Bono remarked on God's heart for the poor:

> God is in the slums, in the cardboard boxes where the poor play house . . . God is in the silence of a mother who has infected her child with a virus that will end both their lives . . . God is in the cries heard under the rubble of war . . . God is in the debris of wasted opportunity and lives, and God is with us if we are with them [the poor].

I get to travel all over the world, leading worship at different churches and conferences. I get to work with some amazing people, I hear inspiring speakers, and I get to see God move in remarkable ways. Recently I went on a ministry trip to South Africa with some friends from Soul Survivor. Compared to most trips this one was fairly low-key. We led at a couple of relatively small evening meetings, but for the rest of our trip we spent time visiting different townships and projects throughout Durban. We spent one afternoon playing football with AIDS orphans. We spent a morning serving breakfast to homeless men. We spent time with a group of children who had learnt to survive on the streets. We visited people's homes, we chatted, and at times we laughed and cried together. During the week my heart was so stirred. I felt devastated at the injustice, and strangely fell more in love with Jesus. In the lives of the people I met I encountered Christ. I can honestly say it was one of the best trips I have been on. There were no big meetings; we didn't see hundreds of lives changed. On the contrary it was our lives that were radically changed.

As we worship, we will change. Beholding is becoming. The more we look to Jesus and spend time adoring Him; the more we unpack the Scriptures to ponder upon His character and nature; the more we will share His heart and obey His commands. Genuine worship will not only lead to our lives, but also our society, being transformed. 'Just as worship begins in holy expectancy, it ends with holy obedience. If worship does not propel us into greater obedience, it has not been worship.'[1]

I love the story of Zacchaeus the tax collector. Intrigued to see who Jesus was, he climbed up a tree to see what all the fuss was about. Jesus looked past the crowd and into the tree where Zacchaeus was sitting and said, 'Zacchaeus, come down immediately. I must stay at your house today.' Zacchaeus was overcome with joy and gladly welcomed Jesus into his home. It's fascinating to read what he did next. Zacchaeus stood up and said to the Lord, 'Look, Lord! Here and now I will give half my possessions to the poor, and if I have cheated anybody out of anything, I will pay back four times the amount' (Luke 19:8). Zacchaeus encountered Jesus and fell in love. His response was to give to the poor – to act justly. We don't read that Jesus told Zacchaeus to do this; it was an impromptu, heartfelt response.

---

[1] Richard Foster, *Celebration of Discipline*, Hodder & Stoughton, 1989, p. 214

Worship is the total alignment of our heart, soul, mind and strength with the will of God. When we worship we will find we are led to the poor, and if we love Jesus we will gladly follow.

John Wesley, the great English evangelist, faced persecution and trials on many occasions. As he travelled preaching the Word of God he was often beaten, mocked and set upon by angry mobs. He faced malicious attacks on his personal character and beliefs. He suffered hardship and pain, and yet in the midst of this he witnessed God doing remarkable things. One time he was asked, 'What is your secret?' To this he replied, 'Each morning I wake up and I set myself on fire for God. Then I go out and people watch me burn!'

Can you begin to imagine the impact we could have as God's people if every morning we looked to God and allowed the fullness of who He is to burn deeply within us for all the world to see? Sadly, as we've seen, contrary to this, we look to ourselves and live lives relying on our own strength. But as my friend Louie Giglio says, 'Attempting to orchestrate the world around us, even for a day, leaves us stressed and spent.'[2]

Trying to light our own fire is futile. Seeking with every fibre of our being to shine in the darkness is pointless. We just can't do it. We are not meant to; our job is to reflect. Like a mirror reflecting an image, we are called to behold and reflect the glory of God. We are made in God's image, marked by Him. Wherever we go, whatever we do, we carry His likeness. Like John Wesley, our role is to burn with the fire that God ignites within us. We need to be consumed with Him. It is

---

[2] Louie Giglio, *I am not but I know I AM*, Multnomah, 2005

Christ in us, the hope of glory.[3] There's a wonderful ease about it. The emphasis is not on us; it is on Him. Our job is to simply behold, and enjoy and marvel. As we do, we are transformed. We embrace our smallness, and glory in God's vastness.

True humility

For many years I thought humility was about completely fading into nothing, in one sense becoming a nobody. The equation in my head was: a quiet person equals a humble person, a loud person equals an arrogant person. This could not be further from the truth. Humility is about having a healthy perspective of who we are in relation to who God is. As John Eldredge says, 'Shame says "I'm nothing to look at. I'm not capable of goodness." Humility says, "I bear a glory for sure, but it's a reflected glory. A grace given to me."'[4]

Humility doesn't stop us from rising up. It doesn't keep us from living bold, brave, adventurous, passionate, strong, loud and exuberant lives. C. S. Lewis captures the sentiment of humility beautifully in his classic book *The Screwtape Letters*. The book is cleverly written from the perspective of one demon to another, plotting to deceive and confuse Christians. One of the demon describes, with frustration, God's desire for humility in us:

> The Enemy [God] wants to bring a man to a state of mind in which he could design the best cathedral in the world and know it to be the best, and rejoice in the fact, without being any more

---

[3] Colossians 1:27

[4] John Eldredge, *Waking the Dead*, Thomas Nelson, 2003

(or less) or otherwise glad at having done it than he would be if it had been done by another. The Enemy [God] wants him, in the end, to be so free from any bias in his own favour that he can rejoice in his own talents as frankly or gratefully as in his neighbour's talents – or in a sunrise, an elephant, or a waterfall. He wants each man, in the long run, to be able to recognise all creatures (even himself) as glorious and excellent things.[5]

What freedom we would feel if we could rejoice over someone else's success with the same wholehearted joy as we have for our own. Humility is not denying the talents God has given us. It means fully embracing every personal skill and success and thanking God for them, but with equal enthusiasm thanking God for the gifts and talents of those around us.

In the poem, 'Our Deepest Fear', Marianne Williamson writes,

Our deepest fear is not that we are inadequate. Our deepest fear is that we are powerful beyond measure. It is our light, not our darkness, that most frightens us. We ask ourselves, 'who am I to be brilliant, gorgeous, talented and fabulous?' Actually, who are you not to be? You are a child of God. Your playing small doesn't serve the world. There's nothing enlightened about shrinking so that other people won't feel insecure around you. We were born to manifest the glory of God that is within us . . . And as we are liberated from our own fear, our presence automatically liberates others.[6]

Now is not the time to shy away. These are days to rise up and reflect. Where are the doctors and scientists who will find a

[5] C. S. Lewis, *The Screwtape Letters*, HarperCollins, 1942, p.71

[6] Marianne Williamson, *A Return To Love: Reflections on the Principles of "A Course in Miracles"*, HarperCollins, 1992, p.190–191

cure for AIDS? Where are the teachers who will educate and love a broken generation? Where are the songwriters who will write melodies of hope? Where are the politicians who will stand up for truth and justice? Where are those who will champion the stewardship of creation? Who among us will father the fatherless? The stakes are high. We need to be a people who inwardly burn with passion and zeal for Christ; at all costs, at all times, and in all situations, determined worshippers in every season of the soul.

Come what may

God is looking for a people who will honour and reflect His glory, come what may. I love the story of Shadrach, Meshach and Abednego in the fiery furnace. The Babylonian King Nebuchadnezzar set in place a new law. Erecting an image of gold, 99 feet high and nine feet wide, the command was issued that when the sound of the horn, flute, zither, lyre, harp, pipes and other kinds of music was heard, all must fall down and worship the golden image. Whoever refused to do so would immediately be thrown into a blazing furnace to die. Shadrach, Meshach and Abednego made their stand and refused to bow the knee. Defiant before the king they declared, 'If we are thrown into the blazing furnace, the God we serve is able to save us from it, and he will rescue us from your hand, O king. But even if he does not, we want you to know, O king, that we will not serve your gods or worship the image of gold you have set up.'[7] Incensed with rage, Nebuchadnezzar ordered the furnace to be heated seven times

---

[7] Daniel 3:17–18

hotter than usual. The furnace became so hot that even the men who threw Shadrach, Meshach and Abednego in were killed.

As Nebuchadnezzar sat down to watch the death of these three men, he saw a sight that startled him. Rising to his feet he asked his advisors, 'Weren't there three that we tied up and threw into the fire? . . . Look! I see four men walking around the fire, unbound and unharmed, and the fourth looks like a son of the gods.'[8] Approaching the furnace Nebuchadnezzar called out, 'Shadrach, Meshach and Abednego, servants of the Most High God, come out! Come here!'

To everyone's bewilderment Shadrach, Meshach and Abednego walked free unharmed – there was not even the smell of burning on them. Stirred by this miracle, Nebuchadnezzar praised their God. In the face of death these three men chose to worship. At great cost to themselves they chose to honour God. Remarkably, God intervened and rescued them from certain death. As a result His name was glorified. And it would have been equally glorified if they had died for their faith, as they were clearly prepared to do.

Graham Staines, an Australian missionary, spent 34 years working amongst the lepers in India, educating the young, and spreading the good news of the gospel. One day in January 1999, Graham and his two young sons were working amongst the poorest of the poor in a local village. With nowhere to sleep, they found shelter in their station wagon. During the night, Hindu extremists surrounded the van and chained the handles of the doors shut. They set the station wagon on fire and fled.

Echoes of Shadrach, Meshach and Abednego. What would

---

[8] Daniel 3:24–25

God do? Would He rescue them from the fiery furnace and glorify His name? When the fire finally cooled, rescuers found the charred body of Graham Staines with his arms wrapped around the bodies of his sons. Through all his many years of faithful service Graham Staines had only endeavoured to serve the poor and help those in need. Left behind to mourn were Graham's wife and daughter, Gladys and Esther. The Indian media descended on Gladys's doorstep to capture her reaction. Her response was quoted in every newspaper across India, a nation of one billion people, the following morning:

> I have only one message for the people of India. I am not bitter neither am I angry. But I have one great desire, that each citizen of this country should establish a personal relationship with Jesus Christ, who gave His life for their sins . . . let us burn hatred and spread the flame of Christ's love.[9]

In that moment the gospel message was proclaimed throughout the nation. As Gladys chose to forgive, to honour God, to ultimately worship, God was glorified and a nation was profoundly impacted. John Piper writes, 'God seldom calls us to an easier life, but always calls us to know more of him and drink more deeply of his sustaining grace.'[10]

In every situation that comes our way, our role is to centre our lives around Christ, and allow Him to glorify His name in and through us. In every trial of life, every circumstance, through battles and blessings, it's Christ in me the hope of glory. We're not called to muster up superhuman strength.

---

[9] Article from www.epm.org/articles/worthy

[10] John Piper, *Don't Waste Your Life*, Crossway Books, 2003, p.178

God doesn't leave us on our own to fight His corner. We're called to surrender our lives to Him, holding nothing back, allowing access to all areas. He is the all-powerful God, mighty to act, the God who has the whole world in His hands. It's as we say 'Yes' to Him, following His ways no matter the cost, that we will see God's transforming resurrection power.

Holding nothing back. . .

When Rick Hoyt was born in 1962, the umbilical cord coiled around his neck and cut off oxygen to his brain, leaving him a quadriplegic. His parents, Dick and Judy, were told that there would be no hope for their child's development. Despite being told that Rick would be 'a vegetable all his life', his parents were determined to raise him as normally as possible. As he was unable to speak, a group of engineers built Rick a specially designed interactive computer that allowed him to communicate his thoughts by using the slight head movements that he could manage.

At the age of 15, Rick told his father that he wanted to participate in a five-mile benefit run for a local lacrosse player who had been paralysed in an accident. Out of love for his son, Dick, who had never previously done any long-distance running, agreed to push Rick in his wheelchair. They finished next to last, but were elated with their achievement. Overwhelmed by the experience, Rick managed to communicate to his parents that for the first time in his life, competing in that race, 'he just didn't feel disabled'. Spurred on by this revelation, father and son, 'Team Hoyt', began entering more races.

After four years of marathons they attempted their first

triathlon – the combination of 42.2 kilometres of running, 180 kilometres of cycling and 3.8 kilometres of swimming. To date they have raced in 64 marathons, with a personal best of 2:40:47; 78 half marathons; 206 triathlons; and they once trekked 6,011 kilometres across America.

This achievement becomes all the more staggering when you consider that when Dick runs he is pushing Rick in his wheelchair; when Dick cycles, Rick is in a special designed seat attached to the front of the bike; and when Dick swims, he is pulling Rick in a heavy stabilised boat that is attached to his waist. Watching film footage of 'Team Hoyt' competing together is phenomenally moving. Driven by love for his son, and a desire to see him fulfilled, Dick has gone to unimaginable lengths to make him feel alive. In every race it is the father, Dick, who does all the work; giving every gram of strength for the sake of his son. Rick cannot offer any physical support – in fact he only makes more work for his father. However, witnessing Dick's affirmation for his son, and watching Rick's face as he crosses the line, you would think that the son had won the race single-handed.[11]

The story of Dick and Rick Hoyt is a powerful reminder of our Father's love and commitment towards us – the Father who gave everything that we might know life in all its fullness. Holding nothing back, the Father delights in us, sings over us, chases after us, cares deeply about us, and sent His only Son to die for us. And what is our only possible response to this extravagant love? . . . To hold nothing back ourselves.

---

[11] www.teamhoyt.com

Survivor Music

Holding Nothing Back: Tim Hughes

Holding Nothing Back is an explosion of energy, expressing a life of full-on worship to God. With tracks produced by Matt Bronleewe (Michael W Smith & Rebecca St James) and Nathan Nockels (When Silence Falls), the songs are epic and exciting. Tim is joined on guitar by Stu G of Delirious? and Lyle Workman (Sting), as well as Brooke Fraser (rising singer/songwriter from New Zealand) on guest vocals.

When Silence Falls: Tim Hughes

A great collection of songs from Tim Hughes, including strings recorded in Prague. Recorded in Nashville, by Nathan Nockels (producer of Facedown and Everything Glorious), and mixed by Sam Gibson (who also mixed Delirious?' World Service). Tim Hughes' lyrics and melodies give you the freedom to sing not only celebrative songs but 'real life' worship songs. Including: Beautiful One, Consuming Fire, Whole World In His Hands and Name Above all Names.

Here I am to worship: Tim Hughes

Tim Hughes has a sensitive spirit, a mature musicality and a God-given gift to draw people into worship. Tim's first studio album, features an outstanding collection of worship songs including, Here I am to Worship (which is now sung in churches around the world), Jesus You Alone, If There's One Thing and My Jesus, My Lifeline. This is a great album full of fresh, invigorating sounds and songs

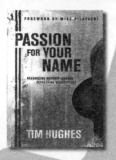

Passion for Your Name: Tim Hughes

Timely and timeless advice for today's worship leader. If you want to be more involved in leading worship in your church, or become a more effective member of the band, then this book is a great place to begin. Tim Hughes looks first at the reasons why we worship God, and why we need to get our hearts right with him, before moving on to the practicalities of choosing a song list, musical dynamics, small group worship, and the art of songwriting.

Survivor books...receive as you read

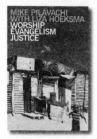

Worship, Evangelism, Justice:
Mike Pilavachi & Liza Hoeksma
We know that worship is much more than singing songs to God. Don't we? This book looks at what happens when we let Worship infuse all areas of our lives, what Evangelism looks like in today's culture, and what God's passion for Justice means in a broken and hurting world. God holds all three close to his heart: if we bring them back together, could we regain the lost voice of the church?

Let the Healing Begin: Jeannie Morgan
Many of us have been hurt by events in our lives – hearts can be broken; feelings of guilt or shame can haunt us. The good news is that Jesus can give us now what we didn't have in the past, so that we can go on with Him in the future. But healing isn't all about receiving. When the broken are made whole they can become channels of God's healing love for others.

Facedown book: Matt Redman
"When we face up to the glory of God, we soon find ourselves facedown in worship. When it comes to expressing our worship, what we do on the outside is a reflection of what's taking place on the inside. Facedown worship always begins as a posture of the heart. It's a person so desperate for the increase of Christ that they find themselves decreasing to the ground in an act of reverent submission." Matt Redman takes us on a journey into wonder, reverence and mystery - urging us to recover the "otherness" of God in our worship.

The Heart of Worship Files & Inside out Worship:
Matt Redman
Advice for cultivating true worship on the inside, mixed in with thoughts and advice as to how to work it out creatively, biblically and congregationally on the outside. Containing practical advice for worship leaders, creative advice for musicians and perceptive insights into the theology of worship.

Guidance from some of todays most seasoned leaders and lead worshippers: Matt Redman, Louie Giglio, Chris Tomlin, Mike Pilavachi, Tim Hughes, Robin Mark, Darlene Zschech, Brian Houston, Terl Bryant, Paul Baloche, Graham Kendrick, Darlene Zschech, Noel Richard, Les Moir & many more.

www.survivor.co.uk